Heinemann EXPLORE Science

Teacher's Book

New International Edition

Grade 4

Tara Lievesley, Deborah Herridge
Series editor: John Stringer

WAYS LEARNING

PEARSON

Pearson Education Limited is a company incorporated in England and Wales having its registered office at Edinburgh Gate, Harlow, Essex, CM20 2JE.

Registered company number: 872828

Text © Pearson Education Limited 2012
First published 2003
This edition published 2012

www.pearsonglobalschools.com

16 15 14 13 12
IMP 10 9 8 7 6 5 4 3 2 1

British Library Cataloguing in Publication Data
A catalogue record for this book is available from the British Library

ISBN 978 0 43513 366 5

Edited by Janice Curry
Designed by Tech-Set Ltd, Gateshead
Original illustrations © Pearson Education Limited, 2003, 2009, 2012
Illustrated by Tech-Set Ltd, Gateshead
Cover photo/illustration © Science Photo Library Ltd
Printed in China (SWTC/01)

Acknowledgements
Every effort has been made to contact copyright holders of material reproduced in this book. Any omissions will be rectified in subsequent printings if notice is given to the publishers.

New International Edition

Introduction

Heinemann Explore Science New International Edition provides a comprehensive, easy-to-use resource written especially for the international primary classroom.

The teaching framework follows the Cambridge International Examinations Primary Science Curriculum Framework (2011), enabling you to minimize planning. The simple structure of *Heinemann Explore Science* gives you flexibility to teach the Units within a Grade in the order that suits your situation.

There is one Unit for each half of a term, with multiple lessons in that Unit. The first lesson in each Unit is an introduction and the last one is a plenary. The other lessons either focus on knowledge and understanding or on manageable, tried and tested investigation activities. The greater the opportunity for investigation, the more practical lessons there are.

Each Grade of *Heinemann Explore Science* contains in the *Teacher's Book* detailed teacher's notes, which provide all the resources you need for planning and delivering successful science lessons. It also includes an accompanying *Student Book* to bring the science topics to life for the children; a *Workbook* with activities to do at school or at home, and six *Readers* to develop students' English language skills through science. Alongside these components, digital resources available via online subscription provide an e-book version of the printed books, opportunities for independent research into the Biology, Chemistry and Physics covered in the scheme and further activities and simulations. For more information on digital resources for this course visit www.pearsonglobalschools.com/explorescience.

This unique combination of science and ICT stimulates students and enables you to deliver enriching science lessons using today's technology.

Heinemann Explore Science and English language development

Science and language development have much in common. In both, students are frequently highly motivated. Science is a popular subject area in primary schools with students (and with teachers!), and produces interesting and engaging results. Language and science are both social activities. Students' language will not develop without co-operation and collaboration, and science is also a collaborative subject. Finally, science experiences can lead, as few other subjects do, to a desire to communicate discoveries.

When developing spoken English, remember:
- Discussion can be stimulated by working in threes. Two friends doing science may have a common and familiar way of communicating. Three extends the discussion.
- Snowball or jigsaw activities, in which groups share and exchange information, are engaging.
- Discussion before and after an investigation can clarify thoughts. Having to explain what students discovered in their investigation helps clarify thinking and improve language skills.
- Presenting results to others imposes a discipline as well as giving purpose to recording and to clear presentation.
- Reading can be developed through following instructions – including safety instructions – and using the *Student Book* and targeted *Readers*.

Students may be understandably reluctant to record their discoveries. When encouraging written recording, use a variety of recording methods.
- Writing to a structure helps to order students' thoughts.
- Annotated diagrams are an effective way of recording practical science – used by adult scientists as well as students.
- A recorded observation alone may lead to a conclusion.
- Ordering and recording whole investigations is difficult, and can often be better done to a writing framework.

Heinemann Explore Science offers and defines new vocabulary. If the words are new to you, or you have any doubts yourself about their definition, use the definitions in the Glossary in the *Student Book*.
- Draw the students' attention to the new words.
- Depending on the students' age, set them to illustrate or define the words themselves.
- Introduce word games – matching the word to the definition.
- Make a 'Words of Science' poster or a class dictionary.

1

- Ask the students to use the words in context; to act them out; to guess which word you are thinking of, either by 20 questions or by giving clues.

- Use cloze procedure to place new words.

Components of the scheme

The **Heinemann Explore Science** *Teacher's Book* provides detailed guidance on teaching with the corresponding sections of the *Student Book* pages. Used alongside the electronic components, where you will find a variety of resources for planning and teaching, the *Teacher's Book* is the main starting point for any lesson. Each Unit provides approximately a half-term's worth of work – an introduction, and almost always four lesson plans (each of which may be taught in a single session or across science sessions during the week), and a final review.

Each Unit introduction provides:

1   Clear background science information to support the non-specialist teacher.

2   Simple definitions of necessary scientific vocabulary.

3   A complete list of resources needed in the Unit.

4   Helpful hints on prior preparation or useful additional resources.

5   Indications of what students should already know and be able to do before starting the Unit.

6   Cross-curricular references to other subject areas.

7   A discussion question to set the scene and introduce a context for the Unit.

There are two types of lesson in **Heinemann Explore Science**. The first type focuses on knowledge and understanding objectives. These lessons contain:

1   Starter activities to initiate whole-class discussion. Questioning will enable you to establish what the students already know.

2   References to the corresponding *Student Book* pages and further information to expand on the paragraphs in the *Student Book*.

3   Safety tips to advise of specific hazards where appropriate.

4   Additional information necessary for the activities in the 'Things to do' section of the *Student Book*, plus suggestions of how to differentiate and record. Any worksheets required are cross-referenced.

5   Integrated ICT research activities using the website.

6   Further details or extra 'fun facts' to support those listed in the *Student Book*.

7   The answer to the 'I wonder...' question, with additional background explanation if necessary.

8   More activities that can be used instead of, or as well as, those in the 'Things to do' section.

9   Ideas for how students could present their work or tips for classroom displays are provided on the website to help students.

10   Suggestions for homework activities.

11   An activity or series of questions to reinforce the main objectives in the plenary session, drawing the lesson to a close.

The second type of lesson offers a challenge to encourage students to use scientific enquiry skills to investigate a problem in context. These contain:

1   Starter activities to initiate whole-class discussion.

2   A challenge introduced in context, explaining what students will be investigating.

3   Safety tips advising of unique hazards where appropriate; an individual risk assessment is always recommended.

4   Further details of how to carry out the investigation, supporting the instructions in the *Student Book*.

5   Lists of materials students will need, including any to be prepared in advance.

6   Explanations of what students should be looking for, or how to keep the test fair. How best to support and extend students.

7   How to organize, record, analyze and present data collected in the investigation. Suitable tables for data recording are provided as worksheets in the *Workbook*.

8   Students are encouraged to review how well they carried out their investigation and how good their results were. Using the report provided for each investigation helps students build evaluation skills by criticizing methods and conclusions.

9 A different scenario is offered to enable students to apply what they have learned.

10 Additional activities can be used instead of, or as well as, the investigative challenge.

11 Suggestions for homework activities.

12 An activity or series of questions to reinforce the main objectives in the plenary session draw the lesson to a close.

At the end of each Unit, material is provided for an assessment and review lesson:

1 A clear summary of the knowledge and skills students have gained through the Unit divided into three levels of attainment.

2 Explanation and expected responses to the 'Check-up' in the *Student Book*.

3 Answers to the assessment worksheets in the *Workbook*.

4 The answer to the original question posed at the beginning of the Unit.

5 A final activity completes the Unit and reminds students of everything they have learned.

In addition, there are six readers for each Grade of the Framework. These are written to match the appropriate science for the Grade, but with close attention to language levels. Students can learn English language through science, and science through practising their English.

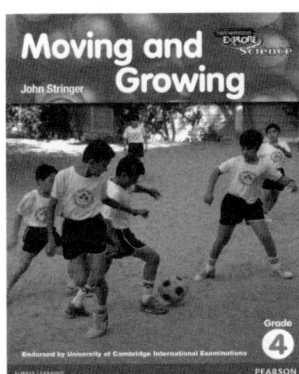

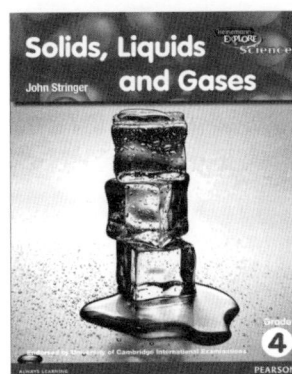

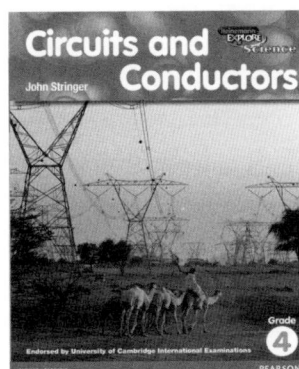

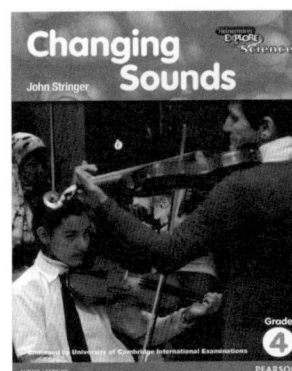

New International Edition

Quick guide to the *Teacher's Book*

The **Heinemann Explore Science 4** *Teacher's Book* provides detailed guidance on teaching the corresponding sections of the *Student Book* pages. Used alongside the e-book, where you will find a variety of resources for planning and teaching, the *Teacher's Book* is the main starting point for any lesson. Each unit provides approximately one half-term's worth of work and comprises an introduction, six or seven lessons (each of which may be taught all at once or across a number of science sessions during the week), plus a review.

Each unit introduction provides:

3 A complete list of resources needed throughout the unit.

4 Helpful hints on prior preparation or useful resources.

2 Clear background science information to support the non-specialist teacher.

5 Indicators of what students should know and be able to do before starting this unit.

1 Useful definitions of scientific vocabulary commonly misunderstood by students.

6 Specific references to other subject areas.

7 An initial discussion question to set the scene and introduce a context for the unit.

There are two types of lesson in *Heinemann Explore Science*. The first type focuses on knowledge and understanding objectives.

3 The answer to the 'I wonder...' question, with additional background explanations if necessary.

1 Starter activities initiate whole-class discussion. Questioning will enable you to find out what the students already know.

2 Safety tips warn of possible hazards where appropriate.

4 Ideas for how students could present their work or tips for classroom displays.

10 References to the corresponding *Student Book* pages and further information to expand on the paragraphs in the *Student Book*.

9 Any additional information necessary for the activities in the 'Things to do' section of the *Student Book*, plus suggestions on how to differentiate and record.

5 Suggestions for homework activities.

6 An activity or series of questions to help reinforce the main objectives in the plenary session to draw the lesson to a close.

8 Further details or extra 'fun facts' to support those listed in the *Student Book*.

7 More activities that can be used instead of or as well as those in the 'Things to do' section.

The second type of lesson offers a challenge to encourage students to use their scientific enquiry skills to investigate a problem in context.

1 Starter activities initiate whole-class discussion.

2 Information on how to organize, record, analyse and present data collected in the investigation. Spreadsheet tables for recording results and exemplar data to convert into charts can be found in the *Student Book* and *Workbook*.

11 The challenge introduces the context and explains what students will be investigating.

3 More activities that can be used instead of or as well as the investigative challenge.

10 Further details of how to carry out the investigation to support the instructions to the students in the *Student Book*.

4 Suggestions for homework activities.

9 List of materials that students will need, including any that need to be prepared in advance.

5 An activity or series of questions to help reinforce the main objectives in the plenary session to draw the lesson to a close.

8 Explanations of what students should be looking for and noticing, or how they should keep the test fair. Ideas on how to support and extend students are also included.

7 Students are encouraged to review how well they carried out their investigation and how good their results were. Use the report provided for each investigation to help students build evaluation skills by criticizing methods and conclusions.

6 Present students with a different scenario to enable them to apply what they have learned.

At the end of each unit, material is provided for an assessment and review lesson.

2 Assessment sheets can be found in the *Workbook*.

1 A clear summary of the knowledge and skills students have gained throughout the unit.

3 A final activity completes the unit to remind students of everything they have learned.

5 Explanation and expected responses to the Check-up in the *Student Book*.

4 The answer to the original question posed at the beginning of the unit. Discuss what the students think now in light of what they have learned.

5

How to use *Heinemann Explore Science*

For ease of use, ***Heinemann Explore Science*** follows the structure of the Cambridge Primary Science Curriculum Framework, 2011. ***Heinemann Explore Science*** has been written so that you can be flexible about what you teach and when.

Heinemann Explore Science is more manageable than many primary science schemes. It has a simple structure, but it also offers wide investigative and research opportunities. A range of engaging tasks is offered for each topic, including practical and research-based activities. Its clear progression and layout offers more support to less confident teachers. Integrated assessment gives indications of how to interpret levels of attainment. There is support for differentiation with suggestions for extra challenges for bright students and support for students struggling with science concepts. There is both experimental and investigative science through reliable practical investigations.

Heinemann Explore Science emphasizes: investigations; the clear use of strong vocabulary lists; building on students' ideas and addressing common misconceptions through questioning and discussion; clearly identified support and extend activities; class demonstration as a basis for some practical activities; and appropriate activities as part of students' homework. It offers flexibility of use; although Units are ordered to match the Cambridge Curriculum Framework, they can be taught in any order to suit a school's own scheme of work. This helps in mixed-age classes.

Differentiation

Within any class there will be a wide range of experience and ability. In a mixed-age class that range is further extended. This is a challenge to any teacher, and many address it through careful differentiation. Commonly, work is planned for a number of different groups (often three: high achievers, a middle range group, and students needing additional support). Teachers then allocate their resources – human and practical – to these groups to ensure the best possible outcome for everybody. This 'planning for differentiation'

is demanding, and may leave feelings of dissatisfaction – 'I didn't spend long enough with the high-fliers/slower group today', 'I hope I'm not neglecting the majority of the class'. Some teachers have similar difficulties with 'differentiation by outcome'. Less able students may be unchallenged by the assumption that they will always produce a few lines of text when others routinely write a page.

Heinemann Explore Science expects that you will need to differentiate your work, and so a range of resources is offered, any of which may stimulate particular groups. You may choose to: present an activity on an investigation table, possibly supported by an informed adult; to set out resources that students can use for creative play; or to use the *Student Book* or *Workbook* for stimulus, for direction or for recording.

The 'starting off' activities in ***Heinemann Explore Science*** invite a third form of differentiation: differentiation by presentation. This is so familiar to teachers that few recognize how effectively they use it. The way in which a topic is presented engages students, but it also enables you to assess their prior knowledge. Because of its practical nature, students who may not shine in other subjects will often contribute more in science. Students who are able in every respect may still surprise you with their knowledge, but this 'knowledge' needs to be probed carefully – a superficial knowledge may lack the depth of understanding on which new science learning can be built.

That's why ***Heinemann Explore Science*** includes a number of exemplar questions to elicit current understanding – whether it is insecure, or even whether students have misconceptions that need gently challenging. It is when you group the students and set the tasks that you 'differentiate by presentation' – an unconscious and instinctive skill that results in different groups busily engaged with differing levels of support and monitoring.

Level statements to help you identify at which level students are working are provided in this *Teacher's Book*, for each Unit. These are also provided at the back of the *Student Book* for discussion and as checklists to enable self-assessment by students.

Heinemann Explore Science contains a wide range of ideas for interaction that includes things to do, questions to ask and resources to support learning. Your professional role is in the effective deployment of those resources.

The Heinemann Explore Science website

This provides a full range of editable planning materials, generic writing frames and presentation templates to support students in recording and presenting their work.

The website also provides digital e-book versions of all the *Readers* for each Grade and for the *Student Books* and *Workbooks*, so that worksheets can be downloaded and printed if needed.

Using ICT for research

Students should develop their research skills using a variety of secondary sources. Throughout the *Student Book*, students are given opportunities to use ICT to research the answers to questions related to the topic of the lesson. At the end of each Unit, a more open question with reference only to the appropriate area of study is introduced to encourage students to develop search skills and strategies.

The Heinemann Explore Science Readers

These have been written bearing in mind the language needs of students for whom English is not a first language. Each book complements a Unit in the scheme. They offer interesting illustrations and simple, engaging text. Word count increases with higher Grades. They can be used as individual readers, books to read at home, or for group reading. They can be used for vocabulary and language exercise, and there are suggestions for activities at the back of each book – from crosswords to team games.

Used alongside the other components of the scheme, they offer opportunities for developing science and language, hand in hand.

Health and safety issues

Primary science is a very safe activity, but that does not mean that you should not consider health and safety issues when you plan, or that you should feel unsupported, either. *Heinemann Explore Science* highlights specific safety issues in lessons when appropriate, and you should also engage in your own risk assessment and take appropriate precautions. This should not be demanding; it involves looking at your students, your circumstances and support staff, and ensuring that you have noted, minimized and if necessary recorded any apparent hazards. It is essential to share this risk assessment with other adults in the classroom.

Every adult on the school site should be familiar with the school's Health and Safety Policy, and especially how it reflects on their responsibilities. They should know the location and proper use of safety equipment. All adults have a responsibility for their own safety, and that of their students in school, whatever their age. This is a responsibility you share with others. Teaching assistants, for example, are often responsible for small groups of students doing practical activities – their supervision may be vital where a hazard has been recognized, for example, when using a cooker. Working with a small group like this offers opportunities not just for realistic but negative teaching ('Don't touch that – it's hot!') but also for positive modelling of safe behaviour ('Now how should I pick this up?').

You can give a very positive image of health and safety issues by performing a routine risk assessment while planning an activity, and encouraging students to make their own assessment of risk, and take their own precautions. Engaging students in safety planning helps them to understand the importance of not taking risks. If students are simply told what is safe without explanation they are less likely to take it as seriously as when they are themselves involved in safety planning.

Here are a few general common-sense reminders:

Food: Eating and drinking is forbidden in school science labs, but some of primary science is concerned with food – science activities may require students to eat, but only with your permission. Fingers do get sucked, and foods are tempting. Ensure that guidelines on 'what to eat' are clear and take into account ethnicity, custom, parental wishes and allergies.

7

Present the best practice in food handling: the cleaning and/or covering of tables, and the use of cooking utensils kept only for this purpose. Pupils should know not to enter the food area unless they are in the practical group (mark or point out an area that can only be entered with clean hands and wearing an apron). Protective clothing not only keeps the students' clothes clean but also prevents food contamination. It should be kept solely for food use. PVC aprons or smocks (coveralls) can be cleaned by wiping with an antibacterial cleaner. Washable aprons should be hot washed at least once a term.

Laminated plastic tables are ideal. Wooden tables (or damaged laminated tables) should be covered with clean plastic tablecloths kept specifically for food. Older students can use antibacterial cleaners after an initial thorough clean by an adult. Spray or wipe all food preparation surfaces including chopping boards with the antibacterial cleaner, wipe clean and leave to dry before using.

Nobody – pupil or adult – should work with food if they are unwell, including sickness, diarrhoea, colds, coughs and other infections. Cuts must be covered with a clean waterproof dressing – blue plasters show up if they drop into food! Supervise students washing hands before food work, or after using the toilet. Provide colourless, perfume-free liquid soap and running water. If a hot air dryer is not available, provide disposable paper towels or paper roller towels. Discourage students from touching their face, hair or other parts of their body, and from coughing or sneezing over food.

Electricity: Teach students about the dangers of mains electricity. Students live with electricity and refusing them experience of it is comparable to not teaching them road safety rules for fear of traffic accidents. Mains electricity has a far greater 'push' round the circuit than battery electricity. It is this greater push that kills. The human body is not a good conductor of electricity, but it conducts electricity far better when wet. Work with low-voltage 'battery' electricity is not risky.

Forces: Many activities in science (and technology) put students at risk because little thought is given to possible outcomes. What will happen if the elastic band snaps, the bag breaks, or the liquid spills? Students may take unnecessary risks too, by not using basic science equipment (eye protection, a cutting board or bench hook)

that could keep them safe. Testing-to-breaking-point activities in topics such as Forces can be dangerous unless students have considered the consequences of breakage.

Animals: The key factor is the welfare of both students and animals. The learning outcome is an understanding of animal welfare and a positive educational experience of (say) a small mammal. It's important to ensure that none of the students has an allergy to animal fur. If you introduce family pets, it's unlikely that they are used to being surrounded by a group of excited students.

Introduce any animal to a group/class yourself. Talk about them, drawing out what the students know, and what they think about how the animal might behave. Students empathize with small animals, and will understand that they could be easily frightened.

The adult should handle the animal throughout the group activity. Students could ask their questions first, and then take it in turns to stroke the animal at the end, which reduces the chances that students will go rubbing their eyes or sucking their fingers afterwards! After their experience, they should wash their hands again, under supervision.

General advice: Younger students can be expected to be able to control risks to themselves and others. They commonly know what is dangerous. Classroom accidents are frequently the result of students forgetting what is sensible because they are caught up in an activity, especially if it is exciting science!

Essential safety advice is contained in a book from the Association for Science Education called *'Be Safe!'* and every teacher should be aware of it and its contents. *Be Safe!* is available from The Association for Science Education, College Lane, Hatfield, Herts. AL10 9AA, UK

www.ase.org.uk
Be Safe! ISBN: 978 0 86357 426 9

CLEAPSS is the advisory service for health and safety in science education. CLEAPSS offers informative publications, a staffed helpline, and a members' website. It is an essential source of science safety knowledge.

www.cleapss.org.uk

Curriculum structure of *Heinemann Explore Science*

Heinemann Explore Science has been very carefully structured to ensure a progressive development in the students using the course, both of scientific process skills and also of knowledge and understanding. This complements the approach taken in the Cambridge Primary Science Curriculum Framework (2011).

The development of scientific process skills throughout the complete course is shown in this skills ladder:

Heinemann Explore Science Science Skills Ladder

Skills Domain	Year 1 Children have opportunities:	Year 2 Children have opportunities:	Year 3 Children have opportunities:	Year 4 Children have opportunities:	Year 5 Children have opportunities:	Year 6 Children have opportunities:
1. **Ideas and evidence in science**	to collect evidence to try to answer a question	to collect evidence to try to answer a question	to collect evidence in a variety of contexts to answer a question or test an idea	to collect evidence in a variety of contexts to test an idea or prediction based on their scientific knowledge and understanding	to consider how scientists have combined evidence from observation and measurement with creative thinking to suggest new ideas and explanations for phenomena	to consider how scientists have combined evidence from observation and measurement with creative thinking to suggest new ideas and explanations for phenomena
2. **Investigative skills** **Planning investigative work**	to test ideas suggested to them and say what they think will happen	to suggest some ideas and questions based on simple knowledge and say how they might find out about them; to say what they think might happen; and to think about and discuss whether comparisons and tests are fair or unfair	in a variety of contexts, to suggest questions and ideas and how to test them; to make predictions about what will happen; to think about how to collect sufficient evidence in some contexts; and to consider what makes a test unfair or evidence sufficient and, with help, plan fair tests	to suggest questions that can be tested and make predictions about what will happen, some of which are based on scientific knowledge; to design a fair test or plan how to collect sufficient evidence; and, in some contexts, to choose what apparatus to use and what to measure	to make predictions of what will happen based on scientific knowledge and understanding, and suggest how to test these; to use knowledge and understanding to plan how to carry out a fair test or how to collect sufficient evidence to test an idea; and to identify factors that need to be taken into consideration in different contexts	to decide how to turn ideas into a form that can be tested and, where appropriate, to make predictions using scientific knowledge and understanding; to identify factors that are relevant to a particular situation; to choose what evidence to collect to investigate a question, ensuring the evidence is sufficient; and to choose what equipment to use

New International Edition

Heinemann Explore Science Science Skills Ladder

Skills Domain	Year 1 Children have opportunities:	Year 2 Children have opportunities:	Year 3 Children have opportunities:	Year 4 Children have opportunities:	Year 5 Children have opportunities:	Year 6 Children have opportunities:
3. **Obtaining and presenting evidence**		to make observations using appropriate senses; to make some measurements of length using standard and non-standard measures; and to present some findings in simple tables and block graphs	to make observations and comparisons; to measure length, volume of liquid and time in standard measures using simple measuring equipment effectively; and to present results in drawing, bar charts and tables	to make observations and comparisons of relevant features in a variety of contexts; to make measurements of temperature, time and force as well as measurements of length; to begin to think about why measurements of length should be repeated; and to present results in bar charts and tables	to make relevant observations; to consolidate measurement of volume, temperature, time and length; to measure pulse rate; to think about why observations and measurements should be repeated; and to present results in bar charts and line graphs	to make a variety of relevant observations and measurements using simple apparatus correctly; to decide when observations and measurements need to be checked, by repeating, to give more reliable data; and to use tables, bar charts and line graphs to present results
4. **Considering evidence and approach**	to communicate observations orally, in drawing, by labelling and in simple writing; to make simple comparisons and groupings that relate to differences and similarities between living things and objects; in some cases to say what their observations show, and whether it was what they expected; and to draw simple conclusions and explain what they did	to make simple comparisons, identifying similarities and differences between living things, objects and events; to say what results show; to say whether their predictions were supported; in some cases to use knowledge to explain what was found out and to draw conclusions; and to explain what they did	to draw conclusions from results and begin to use scientific knowledge to suggest explanations for them; and to make generalizations and begin to identify simple patterns in results presented in tables	to identify simple trends and patterns in results presented in tables, charts and graphs and to suggest explanations for some of these; to explain what the evidence shows and whether it supports any predictions made; and to link the evidence to scientific knowledge and understanding in some contexts	to decide whether results support any prediction; to begin to evaluate repeated results; to recognize and make predictions from patterns in data and suggest explanations for these using scientific knowledge and understanding; to interpret data and think about whether it is sufficient to draw conclusions; and to draw conclusions indicating whether these match any prediction made	to make comparisons; to evaluate repeated results; to identify patterns in results and results that do not appear to fit the pattern; to use results to draw conclusions and to make further predictions; to suggest and evaluate explanations for these predictions using scientific knowledge and understanding; and to say whether the evidence supports any prediction made

Heinemann Explore Science Curriculum Matching Chart for Grade 4

This chart shows where all of the topics and Learning Objectives specified in the Cambridge Primary Science Curriculum Framework (2011) are covered in the *Heinemann Explore Science* course.

Learning Objectives	*Student Book* coverage	Supporting coverage in *Teacher's Book* or *Workbook*
Scientific enquiry		
Scientific enquiry: Ideas and evidence		
Collect evidence in a variety of contexts.	Unit 1: Humans and animals • Growing bones pp.6–7	*Teacher's Book* 4, pp.16–33
	Unit 2: Living things in their environment • Investigating invertebrates pp.24–5	*Teacher's Book* 4, pp.34–51
	Unit 3: Keeping warm • Keeping cool pp.40–1 • Investigating insulators pp.42–3	*Teacher's Book* 4, pp.52–67
	Unit 4: Separating solids and liquids • Solids and liquids pp.50–1 • Changing materials pp.52–3 • Dissolving solids pp.58–9	*Teacher's Book* 4, pp.68–83
	Unit 5: Gases around us • Air in the soil pp.66–7	*Teacher's Book* 4, pp.84–99
	Unit 6: Electricity • Investigating circuits pp.78–9 • Designing switches pp.82–3 • Brighter bulbs pp.84–5	*Teacher's Book* 4, pp.100–115
Test an idea or prediction based on scientific knowledge and understanding.	Unit 1: Humans and animals • Growing bones pp.6–7	*Teacher's Book* 4, pp.16–33
	Unit 2: Living things in their environment • Investigating invertebrates pp.24–5	*Teacher's Book* 4, pp.34–51
	Unit 3: Keeping warm • Keeping cool pp.40–1 • Investigating insulators pp.42–3	*Teacher's Book* 4, pp.52–67
	Unit 4: Separating solids and liquids • Solids and liquids pp.50–1 • Changing materials pp.52–3 • Dissolving solids pp.58–9	*Teacher's Book* 4, pp.68–83
	Unit 5: Gases around us • Air in the soil pp.66–7	*Teacher's Book* 4, pp.84–99
	Unit 6: Electricity • Investigating circuits pp.78–9 • Conductors and insulators pp.80–1 • Designing switches pp.82–3 • Brighter bulbs pp.84–5	*Teacher's Book* 4, pp.100–115
Scientific enquiry: Plan investigative work		
Suggest questions that can be tested and make predictions; communicate these.	Unit 1: Humans and animals • Growing bones pp.6–7	*Teacher's Book* 4, pp.16–33
	Unit 2: Living things in their environment • Using keys pp.22–3	*Teacher's Book* 4, pp.34–51
	Unit 3: Keeping warm • Investigating insulators pp.42–3	*Teacher's Book* 4, pp.52–67
	Unit 4: Separating solids and liquids • Dissolving solids pp.58–9	*Teacher's Book* 4, pp.68–83
	Unit 6: Electricity • Conductors and insulators pp.80–1	*Teacher's Book* 4, pp.100–115
Design a fair test and plan how to collect sufficient evidence.	Unit 1: Humans and animals • Growing bones pp.6–7	*Teacher's Book* 4, pp.16–33
	Unit 7: Sound • How sound travels pp.92–3 • Muffling sound pp.94–5	*Teacher's Book* 4, pp.116–131

New International Edition

Curriculum structure of *Heinemann Explore Science*

Choose apparatus and decide what to measure.	Unit 1: Humans and animals • Growing bones pp.6–7	*Teacher's Book* 4, pp.16–33
	Unit 2: Living things in their environment • Investigating invertebrates pp.24–5	*Teacher's Book* 4, pp.34–51
	Unit 3: Keeping warm • Keeping cool pp.40–1 • Investigating insulators pp.42–3	*Teacher's Book* 4, pp.52–67
	Unit 4: Separating solids and liquids • Solids and liquids pp.50–1 • Changing materials pp.52–3 • Dissolving solids pp.58–9	*Teacher's Book* 4, pp.68–83
	Unit 5: Gases around us • Air in the soil pp.66–7	*Teacher's Book* 4, pp.84–99
	Unit 6: Electricity • Investigating circuits pp.78–9 • Conductors and insulators pp.80–1 • Designing switches pp.82–3 • Brighter bulbs pp.84–5	*Teacher's Book* 4, pp.100–115
	Unit 7: Sound • How sound travels pp.92–3 • Muffling sound pp.94–5 • Changing pitch pp.98–9	*Teacher's Book* 4, pp.116–131

Scientific enquiry: Obtain and present evidence

Make relevant observations and comparisons in a variety of contexts.	Unit 2: Living things in their environment • Investigating invertebrates pp.24–5 • Food chains pp.26–7	*Teacher's Book* 4, pp.34–51
	Unit 6: Electricity • Simple circuits pp.76–7 • Brighter bulbs pp.84–5	*Teacher's Book* 4, pp.100–115
	Unit 7: Sound • Changing pitch pp.98–9	*Teacher's Book* 4, pp.116–131
Measure temperature, time, force and length.	Unit 1: Humans and animals • Growing bones pp.6–7	*Teacher's Book* 4, pp.16–33
	Unit 3: Keeping warm • Measuring temperature pp.36–7 • Keeping cool pp.40–1 • Investigating insulators pp.42–3	*Teacher's Book* 4, pp.52–67
	Unit 4: Separating solids and liquids • Changing materials pp.52–3	*Teacher's Book* 4, pp.68–83 *Workbook* 4, p.38
Begin to think about the need for repeated measurements of, for example, length.	Unit 4: Separating solids and liquids • Dissolving solids pp.58–9	*Teacher's Book* 4, pp.68–83
	Unit 5: Gases around us • Air around us pp.64–5 • Air in the soil pp.66–7	*Teacher's Book* 4, pp.84–99
Present results in drawings, bar charts and tables.	Unit 2: Living things in their environment • Investigating invertebrates pp.24–5	*Teacher's Book* 4, pp.34–51
	Unit 3: Keeping warm • Keeping cool pp.40–1	*Teacher's Book* 4, pp.52–67
	Unit 4: Separating solids and liquids • Changing materials pp.52–3 • Dissolving solids pp.58–9	*Teacher's Book* 4, pp.68–83
	Unit 5: Gases around us • Air in the soil pp.66–7	*Teacher's Book* 4, pp.84–99

Scientific enquiry: Consider evidence and approach

Identify simple trends and patterns in results and suggest explanations for some of these.	Unit 3: Keeping warm • Measuring temperature pp.36–7	*Teacher's Book* 4, pp.52–67

Explain what the evidence shows and whether it supports predictions. Communicate this clearly to others.	Unit 1: Humans and animals • Growing bones pp.6–7 • Your skeleton pp.8–9 • Exercising muscles pp.12–13	*Teacher's Book* 4, pp.16–33
	Unit 2: Living things in their environment • Grouping living things pp.20–1 • Investigating invertebrates pp.24–5 • Changing habitats pp.28–9	*Teacher's Book* 4, pp.34–51
	Unit 3: Keeping warm • Keeping cool pp.40–1 • Investigating insulators pp.42–3	*Teacher's Book* 4, pp.52–67
	Unit 5: Gases around us • Solids, liquids and gases pp.62–3 • Air around us pp.64–5 • Air in the soil pp.66–7	*Teacher's Book* 4, pp.84–99
Link evidence to scientific knowledge and understanding in some contexts.	Unit 1: Humans and animals Unit 2: Living things in their environment Unit 3: Keeping warm Unit 4: Separating solids and liquids Unit 5: Gases around us Unit 6: Electricity Unit 7: Sound	*Teacher's Book* 4, pp.16–33 *Teacher's Book* 4, pp.34–51 *Teacher's Book* 4, pp.52–67 *Teacher's Book* 4, pp.68–83 *Teacher's Book* 4, pp.84–99 *Teacher's Book* 4, pp.100–115 *Teacher's Book* 4, pp.116–131

Biology

Biology: Human and animals

Know that humans (and some animals) have bony skeletons inside their bodies.	Unit 1: Humans and animals • Animal bones pp.2–3 • Broken bones pp.4–5	*Teacher's Book* 4, pp.16–33 *Workbook* 4, p.1
Know how skeletons grow as humans grow, support and protect the body.	Unit 1: Humans and animals • Animal bones pp.2–3 • Growing bones pp.6–7 • Your skeleton pp.8–9	*Teacher's Book* 4, pp.16–33 *Workbook* 4, p.2
Know that animals with skeletons have muscles attached to the bones.	Unit 1: Humans and animals • Contracting muscles pp.10–1	*Teacher's Book* 4, pp.16–33 *Workbook* 4, p.5
Know how a muscle has to contract (shorten) to make a bone move and muscles act in pairs.	Unit 1: Humans and animals • Contracting muscles pp.10–1	*Teacher's Book* 4, pp.16–33 *Workbook* 4, p.5
Explain the role of drugs as medicines.	Unit 1: Humans and animals • Drugs as medicine pp.14–5	*Teacher's Book* 4, pp.16–33 *Workbook* 4, p.7

Biology: Living things in their environment

Investigate how different animals are found in different habitats and are suited to the environment in which they are found.	Unit 2: Living things in their environment • Different habitats pp.18–9 • Investigating invertebrates pp.24–5 • Changing habitats pp.28–9	*Teacher's Book* 4, pp.34–51 *Workbook* 4, p.9
Use simple identification keys.	Unit 2: Living things in their environment • Grouping living things pp.20–1 • Using keys pp.22–3	*Teacher's Book* 4, pp.34–51 *Workbook* 4, pp.13,14,15
Recognize ways that human activity affects the environment e.g. river pollution, recycling waste.	Unit 2: Living things in their environment • Our environment pp.30–1	*Teacher's Book* 4, pp.34–51 *Workbook* 4, p.21

Chemistry

Chemistry: Keeping warm

Know that matter can be solid, liquid or gas.	Unit 4: Separating solids and liquids • Properties of materials pp.48–9 • Solids and liquids pp.50–1	*Teacher's Book* 4, pp.68–83
	Unit 5: Gases around us • Solids, liquids and gases pp.62–3 • Air around us pp.64–5 • Air in the soil pp.66–7 • Different gases pp.68–9 • Moving gases pp.70–1	*Teacher's Book* 4, pp.84–99 *Workbook* 4, pp.33,34,35,36,50,51

13

Investigate how materials change when they are heated and cooled.	Unit 3: Keeping warm • Keeping cool pp.40–1	*Teacher's Book* 4, pp.52–67
	Unit 4: Separating solids and liquids • Changing materials pp.52–3	*Teacher's Book* 4, pp.68–83 *Workbook* 4, pp.36,37
Know that melting is when a solid turns into a liquid and is the reverse of freezing.	Unit 4: Separating solids and liquids • Heating and cooling pp.56–7	*Teacher's Book* 4, pp.68–83 *Workbook* 4, p.37
Observe how water turns into steam when it is heated but on cooling the steam turns back into water.	Unit 5: Gases around us • States of matter pp.72–3	*Teacher's Book* 4, pp.84–99

Physics

Physics: Sound

Explore how sounds are made when objects, materials or air vibrate and learn to measure the volume of sound in decibels with a sound level meter.	Unit 7: Sound • Making sounds pp.90–1	*Teacher's Book* 4, pp.116–131 *Workbook* 4, p.66
Investigate how sound travels through different materials to the ear.	Unit 7: Sound • How sound travels pp.92–3	*Teacher's Book* 4, pp.116–131 *Workbook* 4, p.67,68
Investigate how some materials are effective in preventing sound from travelling through them.	Unit 7: Sound • Muffling sound pp.94–5	*Teacher's Book* 4, pp.116–131 *Workbook* 4, p.70,71
Investigate the way pitch describes how high or low a sound is and that high and low sounds can be loud or soft. Secondary sources can be used.	Unit 7: Sound • Pitch and volume pp.96–7 • Changing pitch pp.98–9	*Teacher's Book* 4, pp.116–131 *Workbook* 4, p.75
Explore how pitch can be changed in musical instruments in a range of ways.	Unit 7: Sound • Changing pitch pp.98–9 • Different instruments pp.100–1	*Teacher's Book* 4, pp.116–131

Physics: Electricity and magnetism

Construct complete circuits using switch, cell (battery), wire and lamps.	Unit 6: Electricity • Simple circuits pp.76–7 • Investigating circuits pp.78–9 • Designing switches pp.82–3 • Brighter bulbs pp.84–5	*Teacher's Book* 4, pp.100–115 *Workbook* 4, pp.52,53,60,61,62
Explore how an electrical device will not work if there is a break in the circuit.	Unit 6: Electricity • Simple circuits pp.76–7 • Conductors and insulators pp.80–1	*Teacher's Book* 4, pp.100–115
Know that electrical current flows and that models can describe this flow, e.g. particles travelling around a circuit.	Unit 6: Electricity • Simple circuits pp.76–7 • Investigating circuits pp.78–9	*Teacher's Book* 4, pp.100–115
Explore the forces between magnets and know that magnets can attract or repel each other.	Unit 6: Electricity • Magnets and metals pp.86–7	*Teacher's Book* 4, pp.100–115
Know that magnets attract some metals but not others.	Unit 6: Electricity • Magnets and metals pp.86–7	*Teacher's Book* 4, pp.100–115

Resources for *Heinemann Explore Science* Grade 4

Science equipment and durable items

balsa wood
bar magnet
batteries (and holders)
beakers, range, including metal and transparent
bottles, glass and plastic
bulbs, selection of
bulb holders, selection of
buzzers
camera, digital or video
clarinet
clock with audible tick or metronome
coat hangers, wire
computers
connecting wires
containers for water and other liquids, different sizes
crocodile clips, selection of
digital balance
electrical conducting materials
electrical insulators
fever strip thermometer
filter paper
fish tank(s) (preferably plastic) for temporary housing of small invertebrates

foil
fossils of bones
funnels
glass beakers
glass bottles (e.g. milk bottles)
hand lenses
household and home-made switches
ICT temperature sensor
light sensor
magnets, including bar, button, ring, horseshoe
magnifying glasses
measuring cylinders, jugs and/or other vessels
microscope
model human skeleton
motor
musical instruments – pitched and unpitched
petri dish or saucer
pictures of local invertebrates and common plants and weeds
plastic syringes, without needles
pooters
recorder

reference books to identify wild animals and flowers
rucksack
rulers
safe white solids, selection of
seconds timer
sieves, selection of
split pins
spoons, range of materials, including plastic and wood
stereo system or loudspeakers
stopwatches
switches, household and hand-made, selection of
tape recorder
thermometers, range of, including ICT temperature sensor
tuning forks, selection of
vessels, selection of
weights
wires, selection of varying thickness
x-ray transparencies

Consumables and items locally available

air freshener
balloons
blanket, old
bark
bed sheet
blotting paper
Blu-tack
bowls
boxes with lids
bubble wrap
butcher's bones, fresh, sterilized and bleached
butter
cardboard
caterpillars
chalks
chocolate, dark and/or milk
clear sticky tape
cling film
clothing, items to test for insulation
coins, copper
compost
cooking oil
cornflour
cotton wool
cake cases
cups, paper, plastic and china
custard powder
drinking straws
drums and drumsticks
elastic bands, varying lengths and thickness

fabrics
felt
flour
foam
foil
greaseproof paper
honey, thick
ice
ice lollies
icing sugar
instant coffee
jam jars
jelly cubes
joining materials; glues, staples, tapes, etc.
kitchen towel
leaves
lemonade, fizzy, in transparent plastic bottle
liquid detergent
marbles
margarine
margarine tubs
materials, selection to test for conductivity
milk
moss
newspaper
paper
paper clips
pasta, dried
pencils, sharpened at both ends
perfume

polystyrene packaging
polystyrene cups
pulses, dried
rice
salt
sand
sandwich bags with seals
shampoo
soap, bar of
soil, different types
sponge
sticky tape
stones
string, thin
sugar
sugar syrup
tape measures
teaspoons
tissue or tracing paper
toffee
towel
tubs, plastic
twigs
vegetable fat, solid
video camera
vinegar
washing powder, non-bio
white powder paint
wood

15

Unit 1: Humans and animals

The objectives for this Unit are that students should be able to:

- Understand why they need a skeleton

- Know that their skeleton is made up of bones that grow with their bodies

- Learn that bones are very strong, but they can break

- Collect and evaluate evidence during scientific investigations.

Science background
SB p.1

Humans and other animals have an internal skeleton, i.e. one that is inside our body. It is rich in calcium. This is the same substance found in our teeth, so providing plenty of calcium as we grow is very important, especially for pregnant mothers, as most bones and teeth are laid down during the early stages of pregnancy. Our bones are continually changing. They do not stay the same, so maintaining a supply of calcium even as an adult is very important. In fact, osteoporosis, the disease which affects some women later in life, is due to the bones becoming 'thinner' or porous.

Bones are hollow but strong. Inside our bones there is a sponge-like substance, called bone marrow. This is where the red blood cells that carry the oxygen around our body in the blood are produced. This is also one of the tastiest bits of the animal as far as wild hunters are concerned! Bones are actually hollow tubes. Hollow tubes are light but strong. If we had solid bones they would weigh the same as stone. We would need much stronger muscles to move then!

Attached to bones are two types of tissue: ligaments and tendons. Tendons attach the muscle to the bone and the ligaments link the bones together. Muscles contract or shorten to make bones move.

Animals that have an external skeleton effectively wear their armour on the outside. Their skeletons are made of a stiff material called chitin. It also has joints to allow the animals to move.

Language

Contract	Get shorter.
External	Outside the body.
Spine	Backbone that protects the spinal cord or nerves.
Vertebrate	Animal with a backbone.

The Words to learn list on page 1 of the *Student Book* can be used to make a classroom display.

Resources

- *Moving and Growing* Reader

- A model human skeleton

- You can use fresh butcher's bones, sterilized and bleached. But you must cut off all sinew and meat. Simmer the bones in a strong washing soda solution. Remove any pieces of sinew still remaining. Leave overnight in a strong domestic bleach solution. Rinse and dry before use. You may prefer to use prepared or plastic bones.

- Fossils of bones

- X-ray transparencies. You can acquire these from hospitals or perhaps a doctor. Names and identifying marks must be removed. There are suppliers that sell transparencies, but they can be expensive.

- Rulers and tape measures

- A video camera

Bright ideas

- Set up a small 'animal farm' to include something like a gerbil or a mouse, some ants or beetles and some snails or slugs. Or ask the students to bring in a pet from home (ask permission first from parents) and refer to it while teaching about the skeleton supporting the body. Make a risk assessment before introducing a pet to the classroom. Consider the welfare of both students and animals. Even the most docile of pets may be excited by a class of children.

16

- Set up a video camera to watch a small collection of different animals moving – those with internal skeletons, those with external skeletons and those without a skeleton. Run the footage at different speeds.

Knowledge check

- Students should be able to name some parts of their body, e.g. legs, arms, etc. Most students should be able to name joints like their elbows and knees. Some may be able to point to their ribs and know that their heart is inside. They may not be aware that their lungs are also under their ribs. Most students think wrongly that their stomach is the whole of the 'soft' area below their ribs.

- Students should know that they need to eat to be healthy and grow.

Skills check

Students need to:

- decide what evidence and measures they want to take

- collect evidence and decide how good it is

- use a ruler to measure distance in centimetres.

Some students will:

- evaluate the evidence to say if it supports their prediction

- be able to recognize that when one muscle contracts the other relaxes and vice versa

- recognize that our skeleton protects vital organs as well as supporting us and helping us move.

Links to other subjects

Literacy: Reading and following simple instructions, e.g. in the measuring activity. Labelling the skeleton.

Numeracy: Organizing and interpreting simple data in tables and graphs, e.g. putting the measurements into a table in the enquiry and producing a graph. Measuring, e.g. using a ruler to measure distance in centimetres.

Information Communication Technology (ICT): Using a digital microscope to observe bones. Using PowerPoint to produce a presentation. Using a digital camera or video to observe animals moving.

History: Find out about bones from animals long ago that have been preserved.

Let's find out...

The Unit opens with this question:

If you break your leg, a doctor puts a plaster cast on it. When the cast comes off, your leg is thinner than it was. Why does the doctor put the cast on? Why is your leg thinner? How have the muscles changed? What can you do to make both legs look the same again?

Discuss the problem. Some students will have either broken a bone at some stage or have met someone who has. The treatment for broken bones has changed in recent years. Instead of a rigid plaster cast that stays on for six weeks, a plastic cast may be used. This is sometimes taken off at night to reduce muscle wastage. Ask the students to think of the broken bones that they have had or seen and how they were treated. Are all broken bones treated the same? Why not?

Unit 1: Humans and animals – Animal bones

The objectives for this lesson are that students should be able to:

- Find out that humans and some animals have skeletons

- Learn that some animals have their skeleton outside their bodies

- Find out what bones are made of

- Present their findings on animal bones.

SB pp.2–3 — Starter

- Dress up as 'Sherlock Bones', with a magnifying glass, muttering under your breath about finding the identity of a dead animal. Pull out of your pocket a huge bone and a much smaller one. Place the two bones on your desk and then look at a selection of other bones on the desk. Hold them up together and see which one matches. Ah ha! I've found a match! Tell the students that the animal was a Triceratops or some such extinct animal. You could cut the bones out of pieces of card. Make everything extra large so the students can see.

Explain

Your bony friend

It's easy to feel the bones of your hand. Students can count them and discover the number of joints in each finger and the bones in their palms. They could draw what they think is inside their hand and compare it with an X-ray.

Bones are alive!
Bones on the outside?

Show a selection of shells. Discuss where they came from. The shell is made of calcium carbonate, similar to bones. It protects the soft parts of the animal from being eaten. When the animal dies the shell is left behind and eventually breaks up into smaller pieces to become part of the sand on a beach.

Big and small

Use the model skeleton to show that some bones are bigger than others. Be sure to tell the students that this is a model and not life-size. Most models are a fraction of life-size and students may think that the model is real – or even a student or small person. Measure the femur (thigh bone) of the model and compare it to one of the students' to see what the scale is. This is a difficult concept for the students to do on their own, but you could do it as a demonstration.

Point out the different-sized bones. Ask students why the smallest bones are not demonstrated on the model. (These are the ear bones which are inside the skull.)

Things to do

I've got one too!

Even using the pictures in the *Student Book* the students should be able to spot the ribs and skull present in both animals. Use either real bones of different animals or some pictures so students can observe that all animals have some bones in common, but they may be in different proportions.

Record

Students could measure real bones and produce a table of results. If the photographs or secondary sources are of a similar scale, they could also be measured.

Students could summarize what they have found out by writing a conclusion to how 'Sherlock Bones' knew that the animal bone he had was from the Triceratops (or whatever animal you mentioned).

Support

Ask students to list the animals that have an internal skeleton. Even looking at pictures of the external parts of an animal can indicate to them that they have legs, a head and a ribcage to protect their heart and internal organs.

Extend

All students should recognize that we have bones of different sizes in our body. Most students will realize that the bones of different animals are differently shaped and proportioned.

Some students will be able to research the names of some bones they see.

18

I wonder...

The legs of animals can be difficult to compare with human limbs because of differences in proportion. For example, the front legs of a horse are made up of the foot and 'forearm'. The 'elbow' joint of a horse is at the point where the 'forearm' joins the body. The dog has a ribcage to protect its heart and lungs, and a skull. You can't see animals' bones because of the flesh and skin covering them.

Dig deeper

The students should find out about the marrow in the centre of bones and that bones are hollow, but strong. Students could also research Andreas Vesalius to find out how he discovered how the bones and muscles in the body are put together.

Did you know?

These facts will remind students that there are lots of bones in our bodies.

- The bones that fuse in a baby are in its head. These are soft plates that are compressed during birth and spring apart once the baby is born. As the child ages, the bones fuse for strength. The fontanel – the membrane at the top of a baby's skull between its skull bones – is often very apparent.

Other ideas

Animal skeletons

Show the students a selection of skeletons from other animals. Discuss how they are similar. Bring in the skeleton of a fish, such as a trout, that you may have filleted. Soak it first in domestic bleach to remove any flesh and to sterilize it.

Many science suppliers provide sets of animal bone X-rays. Use these for identification and comparison exercises.

Presentation

Ask the students to pretend that they are 'Sherlock Bones' and explain how they discovered which animal the bone might have belonged to. Encourage them to use PowerPoint.

At home

Tell the students to find out if everybody has the same number of vertebrae in their backs. Ask them to run their fingers down a friend's spine and count the number of lumps – these are the vertebrae. Suggest they try this out on friends and family of different ages.

Plenary

Discuss with the students what they would look like without a skeleton. Ask them to draw a picture. *If you didn't have an internal skeleton, what might you have instead?*

Unit 1: Humans and animals – Broken bones

The objectives for this lesson are that students should be able to:

- Name some of the important bones in the body

- Discover that bones need to be strong to support their body, but they can break

- Understand how people can look at bones

- Explain what bones are made of.

SB pp.4–5 | **Starter**

- Do a quick brainstorm with the students to produce a list of words to describe materials. The list should include rough, smooth, soft, hard, brittle, flexible, bendy, etc. Show the students a selection of bones and ask them to describe the appearance, texture, etc.

> ⚠ Sterilize bones as described, before handling. Ensure students wash their hands afterwards.

- If you have one, show an X-ray to the class. Have any of the students had X-rays taken. What bone did they break? They may be able to bring the X-ray in to show the class. Discuss their experiences.

- For revision, play 'Simon Says' with parts of the body. You can extend this to pointing to the bones later on in the session and as part of a plenary.

Explain

A dog's dinner

If you have some chicken bones, show how easily they can break. It is better not to let the students do this as the pieces easily splinter. Show that cooked chicken bones are broken more easily than fresh or raw bones. Point out that in the centre of the bone it is hollow and there is some marrow.

Bones are strong

Explain that our bones are made from a material called calcium. It is also in teeth – and in eggshells. Point out that bones are very strong, but they can snap if you give them a sudden hard knock. They can break, like an eggshell. Explain that we can move because of joints between our bones. Some joints are like hinges.

From outer space

Show the students some X-ray transparencies of normal bone and broken bones. X-rays are a type of radiation similar to light. The rays can't travel very far and are stopped by bone, but they pass through flesh, paper and clothes. X-rays are projected from one side of the subject with the film on the other. An X-ray picture shows the bones as white. The X-rays pass through the flesh and develop the film, just as light does in a camera, turning it black.

The area insulated from X-rays stays white. Exposure to too many X-rays can be dangerous, which is why the radiologist taking the X-rays stands behind a lead screen. Lead is an insulator, slowing or preventing the movement of X-rays.

Things to do   WS 1

Looking at bones

Students should use WS 1 to see how many bones they can label on the skeleton. Further research using secondary sources could be used to label more bones correctly.

Record

The fully-labelled WS 1 should provide a sufficient record for the students to learn the names of the main bones.

Support

Some students may benefit from a list of words to use on the board. Everyday names, such as 'shin bone' are sufficient; they don't have to use the scientific names. WS 1 includes some bone names.

20

Extend

Most students should be able to label the skull, ribs and spine.

Some students may be able to label the bones using technical names.

I wonder...

The clavicle or collarbone is the most common bone to break. Falling on your hands transmits the force directly through your arms to this thin bone.

Dig deeper

Bones mend themselves after being broken. The blood and bone marrow flow to fill the gap that is created during the break. This eventually allows calcium to be deposited so new bone is produced. A sprain is tissue damage on a joint.

Did you know?

These facts can be used to challenge the students' preconceived ideas about the hardness/brittleness of bones.

- Although your bones are hard, they are made of 75% water.

Other ideas

Rubber bones

Demonstrate that a bone is made of a similar substance to teeth. Show the students some cooked chicken bones and let them see that they are quite hard and rigid. Place some of the bones in vinegar in a jar. Tell the students that the vinegar is acid like cola, but not sweet. Leave the bones for three or four days. When you take them out they should be bendy and rubbery. The calcium reacts with the acid. The bones that were not put in vinegar should be hard and brittle. This will show that calcium hardens bone.

Video the students bending the rubbery bones and trying to bend the brittle ones.

Make-shift splint

Set the students a design technology task to design a new splint to keep a broken arm still. Ask them to pretend to break an arm. Let them only use materials that they would find in the classroom or that they are already wearing. The splint must be lightweight so it can be worn easily. What sorts of properties does the splint need to have?

Presentation

Students could draw and label a blown-up version of the skeleton to go on the wall.

Ask them to pretend they are doctors and to use the video recording made earlier to help explain what bones are made of. See if they can include the types of food they should eat to make sure their bones receive sufficient calcium, e.g. milk, fresh fruit and vegetables.

At home

Ask the students to write a short rhyme or ditty about the skeleton. If this is too time consuming, suggest they create an acrostic of 'skeleton' or one of the other bones, e.g.

R Round my chest

I Inside my skin

B Being there to protect

S Some of my organs.

Plenary

Play 'Simon Says', using names of parts of the body and also some bones to check that the students have learned some of the main ones.

21

Unit 1: Humans and animals – Growing bones

The objectives for this lesson are that students should be able to:

- Find out if their skeletons grow when we do

- Learn to measure lengths accurately

- Record their measurements accurately and present their findings

- Evaluate their evidence to check whether it supports their ideas.

SB pp.6–7

Starter

- Dress up as 'Sherlock Bones' again, with your magnifying glass, muttering under your breath about having to find out how old the person was who owned this bone. Pull out of your pocket a bone and hold it next to a student's arm: *No! Much too big!* Then next to another student: *No! Far too small!* Then put it next to a third student and state that it is a perfect match: *So this bone is from someone your age!* The bone can be a cut out of a piece of card.

- Explain that bones last longer than any part of the body. They can give us clues about the person they belonged to. *How can they do this?*

The challenge

Read the opening of page 6 in the *Student Book*. Discuss what happens as we grow older, i.e. we grow taller and in other directions. *Do our bones grow?* Obviously, you can't wait for the students to grow to get the results! They might suggest measuring people of different ages. Can they suggest who they should ask to measure?

What to do

To make this a fair test, the students will need to measure the same part of the same limb. This means the first suggestion of measuring students' legs and adults' arms is not a valid one. Discuss with the students why they would or wouldn't use it.

Lining everyone up and looking at the arm lengths is fairer but it doesn't give any data with which to confirm the prediction.

The second option of measuring the forearms of all the participants is preferable. It doesn't have to be the forearm; it could be a shin, thigh, cubit (elbow to tip of the middle finger), arm span or even hand length.

A word of caution: some students might be a little self-conscious about their size. Stress that people grow at different rates – some early, some late – and that everyone does grow!

The students could take pictures of each person they measure or pan a video camera along the line-up of all the participants.

What you need

- Rulers, or any other measuring device, e.g. tape measure

- A video or digital camera.

What to check

The students need to decide exactly where they are going to measure from and to. They will need to make sure that they measure exactly the same place for each person. It may help to encourage them to measure something that has a definite end, like to a fingertip or to a curved joint.

The students should make a prediction about who will have the longest limbs and why.

Support

Some students may need help with reading a tape measure accurately. Practise with some simple readings or provide a less divided scale for them to read.

Extend

All students should be able to tell who has the longest limb.

Some may suggest measuring another limb to check that the same prediction is true for all bones in the body and not just the one they measured.

Some might suggest that it would be better to write down the person's age.

Things to do

WS 2

Record

The students could use the table provided on WS 2 to record their measurements.

Discuss with the students the best way to present data so it is clear and easy to understand. Can they think of other ways of presenting the same data? The students could convert their recorded data into a graph. They could also produce a graph of Class 4's data, given in the *Student Book,* to compare with their own. These are best presented as a bar chart as the data is not continuous. If some students used the person's age to complete the table (this depends whether you mind the students knowing your age!), they could draw a line graph, as the data would be continuous. To help the students recognize whether they can draw a bar chart or a line graph, ask them if there are two sets of numbers in their table. Two columns of numbers will produce a line graph, whereas words and numbers in the table means only a bar chart can be drawn.

Present

Ask the students to look at the chart or graph and 'tell its story', e.g. *The person with the biggest bones is... This is because...*

Encourage them to write what they did, including drawing the table of results and a chart. They might like to take a picture of a 'human graph' where all of the arms being measured are lined up in one photograph to resemble a bar chart.

Ask students to present their findings in groups using PowerPoint. If they used the video camera or the digital camera to record the people they measured, they could incorporate this into explaining what they found out. The pictures taken of the limbs during the experiment could be placed one on top of each other to show a limb 'growing'. Do this by setting the slide show to move automatically.

Can you do better?

WS
3

Ask students to review how good their evidence was. How would they tackle the investigation differently if they were starting

again? Possibly using people's ages instead of classes? Is the evidence conclusive?

Show the students Class 4's report on WS 3. Read it together. *Have Class 4 come to the correct conclusions? What could they have improved? What did they do differently to you?*

Now predict

Class 4E are not measuring people of different ages so they will not produce very conclusive results. The students should suggest that they use at least two different classes in different years.

Class 4W will produce even more conclusive evidence as they will have effectively checked their results by measuring a different bone. All bones will grow as we get older, not just one of them. Obviously, they will reach a maximum when we reach our final size.

Other ideas

Arm span and height

Let each student measure their arm span (from fingertip to fingertip with arms stretched out wide) and compare it with their height. It will vary with individuals.

At home

Ask the students to measure the same limb on students or adults they know at home. Does the pattern still hold true? Are there any differences between boys and girls?

Plenary

Ask the students to draw a picture of how they looked when they were babies and then draw pictures in proportion to show how they have grown to their present size and what they will look like in the future.

Unit 1: Humans and animals – Your skeleton

The objectives for this lesson are that students should be able to:

- Understand that their skeleton supports their body and helps them move

- Find out how their skeleton protects the inside of their body

- Discover how other animals support their bodies

- Group animals according to whether they have internal or external skeletons.

SB pp.8–9 — Starter

- Make two jellies. Leave one to set properly. Put more water in the other one or only let it partially set. Show the jellies to the students. *What do they look like?* They are the same stuff, but one has some support and the other doesn't. The jellies will give them an idea of what we would be like without any bones.

Explain

Jellyfish in the sea

The water supports a jellyfish so that it can maintain its shape. Water is very supportive. We float on water as the water supports our bodies. A beached whale will not live long on land, as its own weight will crush its chest and prevent it breathing so it will eventually die. A shark does not have rigid bones like us, as they would be too dense in the sea. It has flexible cartilage-type bones.

Lose weight!

Explain that we are never without mass but cannot be without weight. Weight is the force of the Earth's gravity on objects. If objects are far from the Earth's gravity – or gravity from other planets – strange things happen. Anything that is very distant from heavenly bodies with their strong gravitational pull becomes 'weightless'.

Explain that all the massive objects in space – the stars, planets and moons – have their own gravitational pull. The bigger the object, the stronger is the pull. The closer a person is to the object, the stronger is its pull. In deep space, the pull is so slight that you float. You have mass – but little or no weight. This has strange effects on you.

- Because gravity squashes the soft discs between the vertebrae, you are actually taller (by 2 cm or so) when weightless. All your bones lose calcium in time and become lighter – a condition similar to osteoporosis.

- Your legs become thinner because there is less fluid in the lower body; a condition astronauts call 'bird-legs'.

Students may not know that it is gravity that shapes our bodies. If we weren't under the influence of gravity, standing upright would be easy – and there would be no need for our large buttock muscles!

Go to bed early, grow very tall...

During the daytime, the discs between our vertebrae are squashed as gravity pulls us down. While we sleep, the spine is allowed to relax, so the discs spring back into shape – hence we are taller in the morning. The difference in measurements will be less than 1 cm.

Things to do — WS 4

Totally spineless

Place a worm on a paper towel and let the students listen to the sound of it moving. Place a snail on a mirror or piece of Perspex and let it move along. Look at the trail. Tilt the glass slightly and watch it moving along. Encourage the students to describe what they can see. Remind them that observation is safely using all of their senses (except taste, in science, of course).

Record

The students can annotate diagrams of the animals to show how they move and support themselves. Alternatively they could write a poem about how an animal moves or supports itself, e.g. an ode to a worm!

Support

Put key words on the board to allow students to describe in detail.

Extend

Many invertebrates actually use a lot of muscles which contract and relax to produce a 'Mexican Wave' effect of ripples.

How strong?

Hollow cylinders can be strong but light. Challenge the students to produce the strongest tower to support the most weight. To make it fair, give each group the same number of pieces of paper, a paper clip and 50 cm of sticky tape. A cylinder is the strongest shape, as the area the mass is spread over is larger than if the students roll the paper very tightly to make the tube more solid. Bones are strong, hollow cylinders.

Record

Students can draw a diagram of the shapes that they made and annotate it to show which shape is strongest.

Support

Give the students two shapes to make so that they make at least one that is bone-like, i.e. cylindrical, rather than trusting to luck.

Extend

Many students should be able to say which shape was the strongest or best at holding up the most mass. (Some students may be able to explain that the hollow shape is strong at the ends, but realize that it collapses easily in the middle.)

I wonder...

This links to the Other ideas in *Broken bones* on page 21. The bone will not rot, but it will go rubbery as the calcium is removed.

Dig deeper

The skeleton has three functions: support, protection of vital organs and to enable the muscles to make us move.

Did you know?

This series of facts shows that different animals have different bones.

Other ideas

Body balloons

Fill up a long balloon with water and make it move across a sloping board. It should creep down the slope. This illustrates how animals without internal skeletons move.

Skeleton model

Give the students some black paper and art straws to produce their own labelled skeleton of the body.

Presentation

Ask the students to work in groups, pretending they are scientists describing how animals without internal skeletons move. Ask them to record using word processing and/or drawing software. They could also work in groups to produce PowerPoint presentations.

At home

Ask the students to make two groups – animals that have internal skeletons and animals that don't. *How many don't have any skeleton at all? What other ways do animals have of supporting their bodies?*

Plenary

Discuss snakes with the students. *How do they move? Do they have internal or external skeletons? What supports them?*

Unit 1: Humans and animals – Contracting muscles

The objectives for this lesson are that students should be able to:

- Learn that muscles contract or shorten to make bones move

- Discover that muscles work in pairs to help us move

- Make a model arm to demonstrate muscle movement

- Research the names of different muscles.

SB pp.10–11

Starter

- Ask students to hold their arms in a strong-man pose. *What happens to the top of your upper arm? What is this bulge?* What happens when they relax their arms? Ask them to feel under their upper arms where muscles contract to straighten their arms.

Explain

A nose like an elephant's

Each of the 40 000 muscles in an elephant's trunk can contract and relax, but only move in one direction. All the muscles combine together to lift a log or make delicate movements such as picking up flowers.

Our muscles are our motors

A muscle is like a machine on a bone. It allows the bone to do something it couldn't do on its own. The arm acts as a lever, although a very inefficient one. Only an external muscle, running directly from shoulder to wrist, would make it efficient, but that would be very vulnerable!

Things to do

WS 5

Contract and relax?

The students should feel the muscle on the upper arm get fatter. It should feel harder. This is the biceps muscle contracting. They won't feel it getting shorter, but this can be inferred, as the distance between the shoulder and the inside of the elbow gets smaller. When the arm goes back down, the other muscle, the triceps, contracts to pull the elbow back down. The muscles in the upper leg are similar but much more complex.

Record

Students can use WS 5 to label a diagram of the muscles in their arm. Can they say what happens when they contract the muscles?

Support

Some students may need help in recognizing that the muscle has got shorter – try measuring it. Also, they may not be able to feel the triceps muscles contracting.

Extend

Most students should recognize that as one muscle contracts the other relaxes, even if they don't use the correct language. This is called antagonistic muscle action.

Some students could try to discover other muscle pairs on their own body. Most limbs or joints that go in two directions will have a pair of muscles to control them.

Caterpillars

This activity can only be done if you have access to caterpillars.

Place the caterpillar on a paper towel and listen to the sounds. Watch it from underneath a piece of glass. Unlike many other invertebrate animals, the caterpillar has many small legs. It does still have a 'ripple' movement but the tiny legs now do the rippling. Six of the legs are true insect legs. The rest are 'false legs' or muscular stumps.

Record

Ask the students to write a poem or ditty about how muscles make bones work, perhaps similar to 'Your head bone's connected to your neck bones'.

Support

Some students may think that the caterpillar must have bones as it has 'legs'. Ask them to watch carefully and see similarities to slugs and snails.

Extend

Most students should see the muscles moving in a 'Mexican Wave' effect again. This is caused by the enlargement of muscles.

Some students may be able to describe movement in terms of lots of different muscles contracting and relaxing. Illustrate this by asking the students to stand in a long line and do a Mexican Wave.

The 'up' is the contract and the 'down' is the relax. Alternatively, get half the class to do it and half to watch so they can describe the process. Then reverse it so all the students see the effect.

I wonder...

Smiling involves the muscles of the eyes and cheeks. Frowning brings in the brow and neck muscles as well.

Dig deeper

We have smooth muscles in our insides, like the muscles that move our intestines, skeletal muscles on our bones to make our arms and legs work, and cardiac muscle, which is almost tireless.

Did you know?

These facts will remind students that muscles are needed to make any part of the body move.

- No one is truly double-jointed. A contortionist has ligaments that are more flexible than the rest of us and can flex their joints further.

Other ideas

WS 6

A model hand

Students follow the instructions, using fine wire or wire pipe cleaners and drinking straws to make an effective model hand.

Presentation

Ask the students to use their models of the hand to show another class how the hand works. They could display their model hands with photographs and X-rays of real hands.

At home

Ask the students to watch their pet or an animal on television carefully. How does it move? Can they see any muscles moving?

Plenary

Ask the students to feel for groups of muscles in their legs. *Can you tell me which ones contract and which ones relax to raise the knee? Describe how the muscles change.* Muscle groups contract and relax.

Unit 1: Humans and animals – Exercising muscles

The objectives for this lesson are that students should be able to:

- Learn that some muscles are working all the time

- Discover that muscles work harder when they exercise

- Recognize that muscles feel tired or ache when they work hard

- Find out how exercise is important in strengthening our muscles.

SB pp.12–13

Starter

- Ask the students to put their hand on their heart. Once they have found it and can feel it beating, ask them to stop it beating for a few seconds. Some students may shout at their heart, some may look like they are concentrating hard and others may say that they can't do it. It is impossible to do. The heart works independently of thought.

- Sometimes we can learn to move muscles that we don't normally move, e.g. one eyebrow independently or our ears. If you can do one of these 'tricks' then perform it for the students. Ask them if they can move any muscles that others can't. Even moving your little toe independently away from the rest is an acquired muscle behaviour.

Explain

Tireless muscle

Explain that the heart is made of cardiac muscle, which is involuntary muscle. Involuntary muscles work without instructions from us. Most of the muscles inside the body are involuntary. We control the voluntary muscles. These are the muscles that we can move at will, like legs, arms and hands, etc. The heart works throughout life, but rests between each squeeze.

Muscles can grow

Through exercise, the blood supply to the muscles increases and they gain more oxygen. This means they can work harder. Muscles can be built up by eating lots of high protein foods and by exercising.

Once you stop working your muscles, your body turns this instant energy into stored energy as fat. Hence, lots of ex-body builders tend to become fat.

Things to do

Exercise

At this stage the students do not need to measure their pulse rate or breathing rate. However, they need to be aware that they change and how they change. The gentle walking should allow them to feel that they breathe and feel similar to when they are resting. However, once they start to do the knee bends, they should notice that they breathe faster and if they place their hand on their heart they should notice that it beats faster. They should feel their leg muscles getting tired.

> ⚠ As the exercise is normal and not too strenuous, there shouldn't be any risk of injury or asthma attacks, but check student medical records and do not demand more than a normal PE lesson.

Record

A simple description of what they did and how the muscles felt afterwards should remind students that as they work their muscles, they become tired.

Support

If the students find it hard to focus on how they feel, ask them to concentrate just on how the muscles in their legs feel. If some students are unable to exercise, ask them to talk to a partner about how they feel. Alternatively, remind them of how they feel after doing PE or at playtime.

Extend

All students should recognize that their muscles feel tired or ache when they are exercised.

Some students could feel the muscles after the exercise and describe how the muscles feel from the outside. They might feel firmer to the touch and warm.

I wonder...

As you work on the same muscles, they will not feel as tired. They become accustomed to the exercise and will be able to do it for longer without feeling tired. This is because they develop a plentiful supply of blood and oxygen for themselves. Muscles feel tired and ache when they are starved of oxygen as they produce lactic acid instead of the usual products of respiration. The process is called anaerobic respiration – respiration without oxygen.

Dig deeper

Hands and feet are amazing because they can do so many things. Humans are one of the only animals with an opposable thumb (one that works against the fingers to enable us to grip things).

Did you know?

The facts here show students that muscles work together to allow us to do things and that different animals have different amounts of muscles.

• The heart beats on average about 300 million times in a lifetime.

Other ideas

Which muscles?

Exercise is good for us. Discuss with the students why, relating it to why their muscles would grow if they continued to exercise. Ask the students to

think of all the forms of exercise they do already and say which muscles they will help to build up, e.g. if you run you will build up leg muscles, if you lift weights you will build up upper arm muscles, etc. All exercise is also very important for strengthening the heart muscles.

Presentation

Encourage the students to produce a poster or leaflet for a local gym or leisure centre. Their posters should mention exercising muscles, why this is good and exercises that people could do.

Ask the students to come up with an exercise that will produce the most growth in as many muscles as possible. They could use word processing or drawing software to help them.

At home

Ask the students to try running upstairs rather than walking. How many days does it take before they are not puffed out at the top and their legs don't ache?

Plenary

Do a quick brainstorm with the students of all the words they could use to describe muscles, their movement and the effect of exercise on them.

Unit 1: Humans and animals – Drugs as medicine

The objectives for this lesson are that students should be able to:

- Learn that drugs affect how their bodies work

- Discover that medicines are drugs that can make us feel better

- Understand why all drugs should be used and stored safely

- Research the use of medicines throughout different times and cultures.

SB pp.14–15 | Starter

- Come into the classroom holding your head and moaning.

- Do the students have any ideas on how you could get rid of your headache and feel better?

- It is likely that someone will suggest taking a drug such as paracetamol or aspirin. *But aren't these drugs? Surely we're not supposed to take drugs, are we?'*

- Begin a discussion on the different words used to describe drugs and medicines. Elicit that 'drug' has a negative, possibly illegal connotation, but that 'medicine' suggests something that will help us.

Explain

Drugs to help us

We have created different medicines to help us get better when we are ill. Medicines are a type of drug and if we take them in the wrong quantity or we give them to the wrong person we can cause harm. We need to take medicines only as they are prescribed. We can buy some medicines ourselves but some we need to get from a doctor.

Ask students what they understand a drug and a medicine to be. Can they name any drugs or medicines? Write down their suggestions on the board.

Emphasize that there are some legal drugs, e.g. alcohol, tobacco and caffeine, and some illegal ones, e.g. cannabis, but that these are not designed to make us better when we are ill.

Redraw your lists into two sets – one inside the other. The larger set is labelled 'drugs' and within this a smaller set of 'medicines'.

- All medicines are drugs but not all drugs are medicines.

Getting better

Ask the students what different medicines they have been given or know about. Be sensitive to students who need to take medicines regularly. Examples that they may suggest include:

- inhaler for asthma

- pain relieving syrup such as Paracetamol syrups for headaches or toothaches

- anti-bacterial eye or ear drops for bacterial infections

- antiseptic creams for cuts and grazes.

Things to do | WS 7

Staying safe

Make a collection of empty drugs packaging – be careful not to leave medicines lying around where students can access them. Ask them where medicines are kept. Look at the picture on page 15 of the *Student Book*. *Why do you think medicines need to be locked away? What other measures are there on the packaging to make medicine safe?* Think about child-proof tops on bottles, Braille lettering, information leaflets and dosage instructions on the sides of packets.

Record

Students can make an information leaflet or a short information film about using medicines safely. Emphasize that medicines are useful and helpful if used according to the instructions.

Support

In small groups, teacher and students should role-play a pharmacist and a patient – the patient describes a common ailment and the pharmacist recommends a medicine and gives advice on how it must be used. WS 7 matches medicines to ailments.

Extend

A visit from someone in the pharmaceutical industry or from a pharmacist would enhance this activity. Students should prepare questions in advance. Remind students that we make medicines for animals too. Think about the medicines we give to our pets or to our farm animals to keep them healthy or make them better when they are ill.

I wonder...

Explain and discuss the saying 'prevention is better than cure'.

Dig deeper

Students can use Internet search engines or libraries to research natural remedies for common ailments. *What plants are grown for their health giving or medicinal properties?*

Did you know?

These facts show students that medicines have been discovered and developed in different ways, throughout history.

- In common with many other medical traditions such as Chinese medicine and Ayervedic traditions, the western tradition has a history of using plants as medicines. Many medicines were made from herbs grown specifically for a medicinal purpose, e.g. peppermint was used to help indigestion, morphine was derived from the opium poppy and used in pain control, ginger was used to relieve nausea and aloe vera was used as a treatment for burns.

- The drug we know today as aspirin was first synthesized by Arthur Eichengrun, a chemist with the German pharmaceutical company Bayer. Aspirin is used to treat minor aches and pains and worldwide we consume about 40,000 tonnes of it each year.

Other ideas

A medicinal herb garden

Plant your own medicinal herb garden filled with plants and herbs that have been used for centuries to combat common illnesses. Make sure all of the plants you choose are safe to consume. Include mint, chamomile, calendula, lemon balm and sage, for example.

Strange cures

The students should role-play a scene of an apothecary or doctor from the sixteenth century. *What advice would the doctor give?* For example, thyme was thought to be a cure for coughs but so too were butter-coated spiders! Prompt students to find out about so called 'cures', e.g. sweet smelling ginger was thought to combat the foul smelling sores of the plague and wrapping a patient in the skin of a donkey was thought to be a cure for rheumatism. *What other strange 'cures' can you discover?*

Presentation

Make a 'Snakes and Ladders' type of board game showing the road to good health. *What tips can you include to climb the ladders to good health? What actions will have you sliding down the snakes towards illness and poor health?*

At home

Research inoculation and the life story of Edward Jenner who pioneered smallpox vaccination. When we travel abroad we sometimes need to get vaccinated against diseases. *What vaccinations are the most common?*

Plenary

Re-cap the actions we can take to prevent illness and stay healthy including adequate diet and exercise, getting enough sleep and good personal hygiene.

New International Edition

Unit 1: Humans and animals – Unit 1 Review

The objectives for this lesson are that students should be able to:

- Check what they have learned about humans and animals in this Unit

- Find out how they are working towards, within and beyond the Grade 4 level.

SB p.16 | Expectations

Students working towards Grade 4 level will:

- State that they have skeletons

- Describe some observable characteristics of bones

- Make measurements when investigating a question.

In addition, students working within Grade 4 level will:

- Describe the main functions of their skeleton

- Describe observable characteristics of bones

- Recognize that their skeletons grow as they grow

- State that movement depends on both skeleton and muscles

- Identify a question to be investigated

- Make relevant observations

- Link evidence to knowledge and understanding

- Explain what has been found out.

Further to this, students working beyond Grade 4 level will also:

- State that when one muscle contracts, another relaxes

- Begin to evaluate the evidence as to whether it answers the question investigated.

Check-up

Discuss with the students what is happening to make Class 4W feel tired.

- The diagram should be similar to the one on WS 5 that the students labelled. They will need to annotate it to show that they understand that as one muscle contracts the other relaxes.

- The explanation for feeling tired is part of Exercising muscles. The muscles need exercise, little and often, so they can manage it without tiring.

Assessment | WS 8

Use the Unit 1 assessment on WS 8 to check the students' understanding of the content of the Unit. The answers are given opposite.

Name: _____ Date: _____

WS 8 Unit 1 assessment

1 Match up these lengths of forearms to the correct person.

5 cm	15 cm	20 cm	12 cm

school student	baby	adult	teenager

2 Label the parts of this skeleton.

3 Look at this diagram of an arm.
  a) Which muscle is contracting, A or B? _____
  b) What is the other muscle doing? _____
  c) How can you tell? _____

Answers

1   5 cm —————— school student
    15 cm ————— baby
    20 cm ————— adult
    12 cm ————— teenager

2   Skull, ribs, spine or vertebrae, pelvis, wrist, knee, ankle.

3   **a**   'A' contracts.

    b   'B' relaxes.

    c   Muscles work in pairs. As one contracts the other relaxes.

The answer!

Refer back to the original question on what happens when you break your leg. The leg is much thinner as the muscles have not been worked properly, so they have started to waste away. The muscles will need to be built back up again with gentle exercise. The cast is put on to keep the leg and the bone straight and still. This allows the bone to be held in place so it can mend itself in the correct shape.

And finally...

Set up a display of the students' model skeletons, both the art straw version and the moveable ones, and their model hands so they can be seen and moved by other students. The students could produce a display of photographs of themselves with their height next to the photograph and a graph of the class data to show that they have a lot of growing to do when compared with you! They could measure other parts of the body as well.

33

Unit 2: Living things in their environment

The objectives for this Unit are that students should be able to:

- Learn that different animals and plants live in different habitats

- Discover how to group animals and plants into categories

- Measure time, distance and temperature accurately

- Understand why natural habitats need protecting.

SB p.17 *Science background*

A habitat is a plant's or animal's 'address'. It provides everything they need for life – food, shelter, a mate and somewhere to dump their waste! Every habitat is demanding and the plant or animal adapts to it. For plants, and some fixed animals, the place where that organism lives is permanent. Plants and animals are exactly suited or adapted to living where they do. That's why they are so seriously affected by environmental change.

Every habitat has food chains to ensure that organisms survive. These food chains represent energy flow; in almost every case this energy originates from the Sun. Green plants capture the Sun's energy and use it to convert water and carbon dioxide to sugars, used for energy and for plant structure. This becomes food for animals.

Plants are the first link in any food chain. Plant-eaters are the next. It is easier to understand this energy flow in terms of food webs. Aphids live on plants and ladybirds on aphids, but the ladybird could meet any number of fates from insect-eating birds, who might themselves take a fancy to a juicy aphid...

There is plentiful plant material for herbivores, and more herbivores than carnivores. This decrease in relative numbers as you go through the energy flow results in a food pyramid – a hawk at the top, a few rodents in the middle, many plants at the bottom, for example.

Students are likely to explore local habitats. This may involve handling plants and animals.

⚠ Students will need to wash their hands thoroughly after touching organisms or rooting around in soil or leaf litter.

⚠ During the topic do not remove any plants from their habitat, as these cannot be easily replaced. Do not pick wild flowers.

There are about a million different kinds of known animals and about 260 000 different kinds of green plants. Names for the same living thing can vary in different cultures.

In the 1700s, a Swedish scientist called Carl von Linné (or Carolus Linnaeus) invented a five-kingdom classification system to make sense of the way scientists group and name living things. The five classifications – plants, animals, fungi, single-celled algae and Protista, and bacteria – are constantly being challenged and changed. He placed living things in groups, according to their similarities or what they have in common: kingdoms, phyla, classes and species. The largest groups are called kingdoms. Plants form one kingdom, animals form a separate kingdom. The smallest groups are species – cows, Bengal tigers or European oak trees, for example. In between are phyla or divisions, classes, orders, families and genera.

Linnaeus gave each species a two-part name. They show which genus and species each living thing belongs in. Latin is used for the names so that they are international. For example, the Latin name for a tiger is *Panthera tigris*. The genus is *Panthera* and the species is *tigris*. The generic name always has a capital letter. The species name has a lower case initial letter.

Language	
Adaptation	How an organism has changed to suit its environment or habitat.
Classification	A method of identifying animals and plants by sub-dividing them into smaller and smaller groups.
Organism	A living thing, either plant or animal.
Variation	The range of differences within a species.

The Words to learn list on page 17 of the *Student Book* can be used to make a classroom display.

Resources

- *Habitats* Reader
- A selection of vessels to collect small animals in, e.g. jam jars or more specialized 'pooters' which allow small invertebrates to be 'sucked' into a small plastic pot

> ⚠️ Disinfect the mouthpiece before and after use.

- An old blanket, bed sheet or towel to catch insects from a tree-beating exercise
- Small magnifiers or hand lenses
- Pictures of local invertebrates and common plants and weeds
- Selection of published keys
- Reference books to identify wild animals and flowers
- Fish tank(s) (preferably plastic) for temporarily housing small invertebrates
- A camera to take time-lapse shots.

Bright ideas

- A digital camera or digital microscope and computer can be used to monitor the movement of small invertebrates. Either use time-lapse or run on double time when watching.

Knowledge check

- Students will need to be aware that plants and animals are living organisms. Use the acronym MR GREEN to establish the seven living processes.

  Movement
  Reproduction
  Growth
  Respiration – getting energy from food
  Excretion – getting rid of waste
  Excitation – respond to a stimulus
  Nutrition – feeding

- Students should know from other topics in Grade 3 that animals need food and that plants make their own food using the Sun's energy.

Skills check

Students need to:

- measure time, distance and temperature

- make observations
- turn ideas into a form that can be tested
- suggest explanations for their experiments using the background science
- be able to communicate what they have found out to others.

Some students will:

- show feeding relationships as food chains
- know a food chain almost always begins with a green plant – some might rightly suggest it begins with the Sun
- recognize that green plants are producers.

Links to other subjects

Literacy: Reading and following simple instructions. Comparing a variety of information texts including IT-based sources.

Numeracy: Measuring and comparing using standard units. Organizing and interpreting simple data in bar graphs or line graphs.

ICT: Using a digital camera. Using a multimedia package to combine text and graphics to make a presentation.

Art: Exploring line, shape, colour and texture in natural forms, e.g. drawing insects and plants.

Let's find out...

The Unit opens with this question:

> *In some countries some people want to protect the countryside. When they travel through it, they take care not to damage it. They plant wild flowers in their gardens. They leave logs lying around. This can look very untidy. So why do they do these things?*

Discuss the question. Throughout the topic the students will learn about the habitats available to live in, how organisms are suited to them and so why we must look after them. Obviously, with the development of land by people, some habitats are disappearing, so we need to replace them. Some students may have noticed these things or have asked their parents about them.

Unit 2: Living things in their environment – Different habitats

The objectives for this lesson are that students should be able to:

- Find out about different habitats in which animals and plants live naturally

- Learn why plants and animals survive best in their own habitat

- Recognise different habitats and understand why they suit the living things that grow there

- Plan or make a wildlife habitat for your school grounds.

SB pp.18–19   *Starter*

- Show some pictures, such as desert plants, the rainforest, polar scenery and the seashore, to illustrate different habitats. Discuss what they show and what sort of things you find there. *Can you describe the habitats?*

- Wear a thick jumper, scarf, gloves, etc. Alternatively, if you have motorbike leathers, a wet suit or ski suit, wear those – in fact, anything the students will not expect you to wear! *What's wrong with my outfit?* The students should be able to tell you that it's too hot/cold/not enough snow/water for those clothes. Discuss why you would wear these clothes. *Do animals dress up to suit where they live? How do they survive in their habitats?*

Explain

Where should we live?

Animals and plants live where they do because they are adapted to the conditions. Humans have learned to dress and house themselves so they can live almost anywhere.

Camels store fat, not water, in their hump. It provides them with a source of food and liquid especially for when there is none close by. The camel's spine is not humped though! Camels have very large feet so they don't sink in the sand. This gives them a large surface area to spread their weight over – like snow shoes.

Penguins have a waterproof skin and a layer of fat to keep them warm. They also huddle together to keep warm.

Are you in the habit?

The word 'habitat' stems from the Latin for 'dwell'. A habit is something you do regularly. A habitat is a place that you go back to regularly that provides you with food and shelter.

Things to do

Let's investigate habitats

The general types of habitat that you might find around the school are ponds, long grass, short grass, damp soil, under steps, under trees and shrubs.

Well in advance, set up a shallow dish of water outside as a mini pond. Students will be amazed at what it attracts.

The students will need to give each habitat a name, e.g. its location in the school grounds, or a number and describe the conditions there.

> ⚠ If you plan to take the students on a trip outside the school grounds, parental consent must be in line with school guidelines. Students with allergies, including hay fever, should have medication available.

Record

The students could produce a map of the school grounds with labels for each habitat and then a key outlining the conditions in each.

Support

Give the students some describing words to use for their habitats. A list of bullet points would suffice.

Extend

All students should recognize that not all areas of the grounds are the same.

Some students may write detailed descriptions of the habitats they discover.

Where do you live?

This activity follows on from the previous one, although it can stand alone. Students are asked to use prior knowledge on where they might find certain animals which they can easily recognize. It also encourages them to think about why they might find these animals there.

> ⚠ See above.

Record

If the students prepared a map for the previous activity, they could add the names of any plants and animals they found in those habitats.

Support

Some students may need help with finding the animals, especially if they are not quiet or patient.

Extend

All students should recognize that a snail will be found where it is damp.

Some students will be able to observe some plants found in their habitats.

Dig deeper

Students should find out more about habitats and biomes, which are areas or zones of the world that have different climates. Obviously, a camel couldn't survive in a polar habitat because the camel is not adapted to the cold.

Did you know?

These facts illustrate that animals adapt to their habitat.

I wonder...

The students should recognize that a pond is being described. In the pond, they might find fish, frogs, newts, water boatmen and water beetles. Plants might include Canadian pondweed, water lilies and duckweed.

Other ideas

Your own habitat

Set up a wildlife area for long-term use. It is far simpler than you think! Choose an area that is least disturbed by people. If it has grass, arrange for it to be left long and regularly watered. Then scatter some wild flower seeds over the ground. Even without grass, the area can still be turned into some interesting habitats. Use plant pots turned upside down, propped up with some twigs, so that small creatures can get underneath. Put some moss or leaf litter under them. Leave some piles of twigs in a corner and place some soil around the edges. This should encourage insects. Hang bird feeders outside the classroom windows to encourage a range of birds. Put some seeds on the ground, some on a table and some in the feeder.

Presentation

Ask students to work in groups to prepare a PowerPoint presentation. Encourage them to import pictures from the Internet onto their slides. Ask the students to pretend they belong to a local nature conservation group and to present a 'virtual' tour of the habitats in the school area.

At home

WS 9

Ask the students to look around their habitat and describe it as a 'for sale' sign. Remind them that a habitat is a place that provides shelter and food.

Ask students to complete WS 9.

Plenary

Show some of the pictures referred to in the Starter activity and ask the students to predict what sort of animals would live there. They will probably find it harder to think of plants, but they should have a go. Set them the challenge of finding out for the next lesson.

Unit 2: Living things in their environment – Grouping living things

The objectives for this lesson are that students should be able to:

- Understand that there are similarities and differences between animals

- Discover how plants and animals can be grouped by features they have in common

- Design your own groups for plants and animals

- Present your plant and animal groups using ICT.

SB pp.20–21

Starter

- Carolus Linnaeus (originally Carl von Linné) was the first person to put plants and animals into groups or classes. He put similar ones in the same groups. We still use his system today. Do the students know which groups animals are divided into? *Which group are humans in?*

- Take a group of objects into the classroom, such as cuddly toys, cutlery, hair decorations, etc. How are they similar and how are they different? Then silently place them in groups. Ask the students to guess how you are grouping them. Change the groups and repeat the question.

- Take a variety of animal pictures into the classroom and do the same with them.

Explain

How are they different?

Students will find it easy to spot the differences between different animals and plants, but much harder to spot similarities. Differences like size and colour are not as important as differences in structure. Encourage them to group animals by similarities. *How are these two animals alike?*

The same but different

There are five main kingdoms for classification – plants, animals, fungi, single-celled algae and Protista, and bacteria. Animals are further split into vertebrates and invertebrates (animals with and without a backbone).

Vertebrates are then split into mammals, birds, amphibians, reptiles and fish.

Plants are divided into those that flower and those that don't.

Plants and animals are also classified by internal features. E.g. dinosaurs are classified by the structure of their hips. Their difference may not be immediately obvious.

The groups get smaller and smaller until you reach the species. A lot of the reasoning behind naming an organism is based on its evolutionary origin.

Things to do

What are you like?

Give the students a selection of pictures of small organisms and plants for them to group. The students should group the organisms by observable features, e.g. the animals by the number of legs or wings and the plants by the colour or shape of the flower. The students need to say how they sorted them out and then try a different method of sorting.

Record

Drawing the organisms will take time, but a picture or diagram of the groupings they had with an explanation of the reasoning behind them will remind students of what they did.

Support

If using pictures of organisms doesn't give enough 'big' differences, try using pictures of people with obvious differences in appearance, e.g. facial feaures, hair length or colour. Sort the whole class into groups – those with lighter hair and those with darker hair, then into gender, etc. This will illustrate how it is possible to group things in different ways. It's important not to classify people by changeable features – clothes, glasses, etc.

Extend

Most students should be able to say how they grouped their objects.

Some students will be able to change their groupings. Faster workers could try to split their groups into smaller ones, by subdividing them, e.g. animals with legs, animals without legs, then splitting the animals with legs into small groups based on the number of legs. Ask them to explain what they have done.

I wonder...

A whale is a mammal because it gives birth to live young and feeds them on milk. It doesn't have any gills and breathes air, unlike a fish.

Dig deeper

Latin is the international language used to name plants and animals. Whtever the local name, the plant or animal's Latin name is international.

Carl von Linné even changed his own name to a Latin version: Carolus Linnaeus.

Did you know?

These facts will remind students that animals that might be different can be related to one another and animals have not always been known by the names they have today.

Other ideas | WS 10 | WS 11

Quick identification

Ask students to think about what it is that allows them to recognize an animal or plant correctly. Students often identify one organism and then classify all the others by how much they resemble it. Get them to look more widely than this. Students should use WS 10 to describe these organisms and the features they use to recognize them by.

Pair work

Students should fill in the animal and plant data on WS 11, then swap *Workbooks* with a partner. Without knowing the name of the organism or plant, the students have to draw a picture to match the information on the WS.

Presentation

The students can work together to use word processing software to write about how they would place a new organism in a group (by an observable feature). If they have used a database or the spreadsheet in one of the above activities they could incorporate this into the presentation.

The students could also produce a 'passport' for each organism, including information on where they live, what they look like and any distinguishing marks, etc. Mount these on a wall to create a large display or even incorporate them by placing them on the map of the school grounds which you might already have on display.

Some animals and plants have common names rather than the scientific Latin to identify them. Find some pictures of interesting plants and animals that the students may not know and ask them to invent a common name for them based on their observable characteristics.

At home | WS 12

Invite students to draw their version of a 'cameleopard' and to describe where it could live and what features it would have.

Ask students to complete WS 12. This confirms their understanding of the vertebrate groups and the ways in which camels as a group are adapted to a desert habitat. The wide feet prevent sinking, the eyelashes keep sand out, the hump carries food and water reserves. Desert animals like the jerboa have similar adaptations.

Plenary

Show some leaves from trees, including evergreens and fir trees. Ask the students to group them and say how they were grouped. Encourage them to describe the observable features.

39

Unit 2: Living things in their environment – Using keys

The objectives for this lesson are that students should be able to:

- Learn that animals and plants can be identified by their features

- Create and use a key to identify some animals and plants

- Use their keys on other students to test how well they work

- Make up a name for an animal so that people can identify it from the name.

SB pp.22–23   Starter

- Use the same group of objects as in the Starter for *Grouping living things* and ask the students to group them. This revises the work from the last lesson which leads into actually identifying the object even if it is unknown. Introduce an object that fits in with one of the groups but that the students might not have seen before, e.g. a cuddly snake or a pair of chopsticks. *Does this belong in any of the groups? What is different about it? How would you describe it?* The students should still be able to identify it as a toy/cutlery, even though it is totally different from the others.

Explain

Unlocking

Prepare a key to unlock the identity of the organism or object. Ask the students to try to split the objects into smaller and smaller groups until there is only one object in the group. As they do this, write down on the board all the ways they separated the objects.

What's my name?

This activity shows that there are two types of key. The arrow or branching key 2 is easier to follow as it is simple 'yes' or 'no' answers. The questions and 'go to' key 1 are generally used for more able older students.

Things to do   WS 13

What am I?

Collecting the animals from a habitat takes great care and patience. If possible, observe them in situ and then take the notes on their features back to the classroom. Collecting animals takes time, but it is fun for the students. As long as you instruct them how to do this carefully, it is also harmless to the animals.

Set some yoghurt pots into small depressions in the ground. Protect them from rain if necessary. These 'pitfall' traps should collect a variety of animals.

Shrub or tree 'beating' also yields a range of organisms. Hold a sheet or towel under a branch and move the branch about gently. The sheet should catch anything that falls out.

Using pooters to 'suck' an animal into its own pot is not as easy as it looks. Students might worry about breathing in or swallowing the animal! Reassure them that the pooters have a gauze on the end to stop this happening. Gently use soft paintbrushes to transfer animals to a holding container.

Branching keys are made of simple questions that have 'yes' or 'no' answers. Devising this type of question takes practice. Practise with the students by pairing them up and let them ask each other questions that have only 'yes' or 'no' answers.

Give each student a copy of WS 13 to help them identify some minibeasts using a branching key.

Record

To clarify that they have followed the key properly, let the students write down the path that they followed to identify the organism.

Support

Identifying the animals involves looking at the observable features. Ask students to make comparisons between pairs of animals.

Extend

Most students should be able to identify the animals in a given key.

Creating a key is not easy. The hardest part, once they have mastered the art of asking yes/no questions, is deciding the order in which to ask the questions. The first question should be one that splits the animals into the two or three largest groups like, 'Does it have six legs?'

Some students will be able to produce their own key by asking the simple yes or no questions.

Dig deeper

Darwin travelled on the *Beagle* to the Galapagos islands and discovered that species of finches were slightly different on each island due to the conditions they lived in. He also observed that tortoises had different neck lengths for eating the leaves at different heights.

I wonder...

Students should realize that to give an animal a name they need to make sure it is grouped properly first. This will depend not only on its observable features, but also on other animals to which it is related.

Did you know?

These facts will remind students that plants that might be different can be related to each other.

Other ideas

WS 14

Use WS 14 to reinforce understanding of a branching key and to encourage invention of a new one.

Computer programs are also available with branching keys that set up the key structure for you as you type in the questions.

Presentation

Ask students to pretend they are botanists or zoologists and work in groups to prepare a PowerPoint presentation that shows how they identified an unknown animal or plant. They should explain all the questions they asked to construct their key.

The students could produce a large-scale key to display on a wall. You could refer to it later for identification purposes.

At home

WS 15

Ask students to write some yes or no questions about their family or people they know and then to produce a key to identify them.

Ask students to complete WS 15, using it to identify the friends.

Plenary

Bring in a leaf from a tree and use a published key that identifies trees. Look at the leaf together and discuss what the tree might be. Then use the key to identify the type of tree the leaf comes from.

Alternatively, ask the students to help you make a key to identify a selection of leaves from trees. This will help to reinforce the fact that plants as well as animals are identified by observable features.

Unit 2: Living things in their environment – Investigating invertebrates

The objectives for this lesson are that students should be able to:

- Prepare a suitable habitat for invertebrates

- Investigate what conditions invertebrates like to live in

- Make a reliable observation of their invertebrates

- Explain their evidence scientifically.

SB pp.24–25

Starter

- If possible, bring in an empty fish tank and a goldfish in a bag. Alternatively, show the students a picture of fish in a tank. *Will the fish manage in the tank?* Obviously a dolphin won't fit, but a trigger-fish might. Tell the students that you have decided to try giving the fish more air and therefore you won't be putting any water in. *How will it cope?* The students should say that the fish will die. *What should we do?*

Consult your school's guidelines before keeping animals like goldfish or gerbils in the classroom. Health and safety rules must be followed, but these are not onerous. Such animals can be kept in a classroom successfully for several years. Handling the animals and cleaning should be done by an adult, but feeding and observing are jobs for the students.

The challenge

Read the opening of page 24 in the *Student Book*. Discuss the different ways Class 4 are going to use to find out what conditions the invertebrates choose. *Which one would be best?* Counting whether the invertebrates are still there or alive, is not going to produce any decent results that can be analysed. Counting the invertebrates at the end of the day is helpful, as a bar chart can be produced from this data. Using a video camera or a digital camera for photographs are both excellent if you want to incorporate the information into a display or presentation. They don't give any data to look

at unless you count the invertebrates in each area after each picture.

What to do

The challenge is to find out what conditions or habitat the invertebrates would like to live in. Providing a variety of conditions within a fish tank keeps the invertebrates manageable. The students can collect the leaf litter, soil and twigs, etc. and place them in different areas of the tank.

What you need

- Small invertebrates – collect a pile of leaf litter and you should find some easily

- A fish tank – one would suffice but as plastic ones are quite cheap, you could have a couple

- Soil, leaves and twigs, etc. for the conditions

- A digital camera or video camera to take time-lapse shots

What to check

Ensure that all the invertebrates are released at the same time in the same place. If you are setting up more than one tank, the number of invertebrates in each tank should be the same. The time they are given to find their selected habitat should also be the same for all invertebrates. Make sure all the invertebrates are alive before you start the activity!

Support

Some students will want to move the contents of the tank about immediately to see where the invertebrates have gone. Point out that they do need to be left alone. If the students are so interested that they don't want to leave the tank alone, let them watch for 15 minutes and note down the movements of the invertebrates.

Extend

All students should be able to say where the most invertebrates were found at the end of the experiment and therefore state the habitat they select.

Some students could set up another enquiry with a variety of leaves to determine which leaves or barks the invertebrates select.

What did you find? WS 16 WS 17

The students should use the table provided on WS 16 to record the number of invertebrates found and to produce a graph.

Ask the students to draw their conclusions from their investigation using WS 17.

Present

Ask the students to look at the chart or graph and use it to explain the invertebrates' choices.

Let students present their findings in groups using the speeded-up video.

Can you do better?

Show the students Class 4's report and read it together. *Were Class 4 detailed enough in their observations? Did they look carefully or not?* In fact, they didn't because they assumed that the invertebrates had escaped as they didn't count the 30 invertebrates back in again.

Now predict

Discuss where the invertebrates would usually be found, i.e. underneath the damp leaves or bark. This is the information that the students should want to give to Class 3.

Centipedes are likely to be found in damp places out of the way of sunlight. This is partly because they eat slugs and worms, which also live in these conditions.

It is best to use lots of invertebrates as the results will be more conclusive.

Other ideas

Snails

If you can't find other invertebrates, then snails are a good choice as they are easy to see. Put a small sticky label on each shell to identify them and watch their movements, especially if using a digital or video camera. Take the label off when it's time to return the snail to its home.

Ant and worm farms

You can buy both ant farms and worm farms. They are easy to set up and being small, with glass or plastic sides, they enable students to see the tunnels that they dig for their homes.

At home WS 18

Ask the students to hunt for wildlife habitats at home or in a local park. How many different organisms can they find in one habitat they look at? Even under a plant pot there will be a couple of small invertebrates and a spider or two.

Ask students to complete WS 18.

Plenary

It is essential that students explain their discoveries. They should link them to their understanding, e.g. the invertebrates were mainly found underneath the leaves and the bark as they provide them with shelter and food. Did they discover anything unusual?

Unit 2: Living things in their environment – Food chains

The objectives for this lesson are that students should be able to:

- Learn that some animals eat other animals to give them energy

- Find out that a food chain shows who eats who, or what, in a habitat

- Discover which animals are predators and which are prey

- Present or role play a food chain in action.

SB pp.26–27 — Starter

- Take in some green plants or parts of plants that we eat. *What other animals eat plants like these?* Discuss some animals that eat other animals, e.g. lion eat buffalo. *What does the buffalo eat?* Discuss some other food chains, both from known habitats and more unusual ones.

- Ask the students to tell you any food that they eat. Tell them that you can prove that everything they eat is really green plants. This is quite simple, e.g. if they say chickenburger and fries, then the burger comes from a chicken, the chicken eats grain and grain is the seed of plants.

Explain

Where does energy come from?

Almost all energy originates from the Sun, as green plants use the Sun's energy to photosynthesize and produce sugars that are stored as starch in their leaves. This starch is the food that animals eat. At this level, the students need to be aware that all their food comes from green plants.

Predator and prey

All food chains start with a producer that produces the food eaten by a consumer. For example, plankton is a producer, a fish is a consumer, but so is the penguin that eats the fish. The fish is called a primary consumer to distinguish it from the penguin, which is the secondary consumer.

The fish is also the prey of the penguin, which is its predator. The fish has other predators, like humans. We are generally a top predator.

Things to do — WS 19

Short and simple

The arrows in a food chain always follow the direction of energy flow from the Sun. They do not show who eats who, but who gives the energy to whom. One way to remember this is that the arrows always point to the animal that does the eating! This is the direction of the energy flow.

Record

Students should complete WS 19.

Students could also use pictures from magazines or computer-generated pictures to produce a pictorial version of food chains. Labels should indicate producer, predator and prey.

Support

Some students may need to see pictures of animals to see which animal eats what. Ask the students to identify the consumers, predators and prey as well as producers.

Extend

Most students should be able to recognize the predator and prey in a food chain. All students should know that food chains normally start with the Sun and a green plant.

Some students may be able to link food chains to make food webs. A food web is a collection of food chains that have some organisms in common.

Dig deeper

There is also information on food webs and pyramids of numbers. While this information will be covered in more depth later on, introducing it now will enable more able students to progress further.

I wonder...

Students are asked to recall what they learned about plants in Grade 3. All green plants get their energy from the Sun.

Did you know?

These facts illustrate that similar animals can eat very different things.

Explain to students that some animals have adapted to eat some remarkable foods, e.g. a snake can dislocate its whole jaw to eat large rodents.

Other ideas

Snails' pace

Try setting up a snail race to see which food the snail wants to eat. Place some foods on a small shiny piece of paper at one end of a table and some snails at the other end. This is great fun for the students to watch, although it is a slow process! Try using lettuce, Hosta leaves and carrots.

The students could design a race board for the snails in design technology.

Presentation

Ask the students to work in groups to prepare a PowerPoint presentation to show who eats who in various food chains.

Encourage the students to produce a drama or role-play, dressing up or giving themselves labels to show who or what they would eat and why. The role-play should show a food chain in action.

At home

WS 20

Ask the students to produce a food chain of what they eat for their dinner. They should find that they are at one end of the food chain and, hopefully, a green plant is at the other end.

Ask students to complete WS 20, which is a food chain game.

Plenary

Show the students a collection of pictures of animals and plants and ask them to produce a food chain that uses as many of the pictures as possible. Ask them which are the predators and which the prey.

45

Unit 2: Living things in their environment – Changing habitats

The objectives for this lesson are that students should be able to:

- Learn how and why animals and plants are adapted to their habitat

- Find out that some animals, including humans, can adapt to different habitats

- Understand why living things and their habitats need protecting

- Make a plan to reduce how they affect and damage their environment.

SB pp.28–29 — Starter

- Show a picture of penguins. *These are birds but how are they different from sparrows, for example? Why?* Do the same by comparing a picture of a shark with a goldfish.

- Dress up in a different set of clothes, e.g. wear summer clothes in winter or vice versa. Ask the students what you have done. This will illustrate that we can change to suit the conditions we live in. Explain that over millions of years animals have also changed to suit their conditions or habitats, by the process called evolution.

Explain

All change

All cats have claws that can be retracted, have pointed canines and have pointed ears. If you look at a variety of cats, they all have similar faces. When cats are watching their prey, their heads stay still as they slink along the grass.

Do you want to visit my place?

The cartoon illustrates that a rabbit couldn't live in a pond. A discussion with the students should show that they know a fish can't live out of water and that most animals would die in a pond. Make a few more suggestions about animals living in silly places. Ask the students what features about the animal or plant make it suitable for living where it does. This refers back to Different habitats.

Things to do

Save our habitat

The students need to understand that a habitat needs to be looked after to provide the shelter and food for the organisms living there. If the habitat is damaged, they will have nowhere to live. *What would happen if your house burnt down?* This should give them an idea of the devastation caused by destroying a habitat.

Not all habitats are attractive. Make a case for damp, dark places.

Support

Collect and use vocabulary describing different habitats.

Extend

Most students should recognize that the habitat that an organism lives in has to be cared for. Some could produce a leaflet or poster to advertise the necessity of saving a habitat.

I wonder...

Recycling bottles, newspapers and magazines will help reduce the number of trees that need to be cut down. Turning lights off when they aren't needed will reduce the amount of electricity we need and so cut down not only on fuel bills, but also save some of the fossil fuels that are burnt to produce electricity.

Dig deeper

Students should look for information on different ways that habitats are damaged and how some animals have changed to suit their environment.

Did you know?

Facts in this sequence remind students that we need to protect the environment and recycle to save parts of it.

Other ideas

Use it again

Ask the students to design packaging that could be re-used. They could do this on the computer or in design technology. The students will need to consider which materials they could use that can be recycled.

Permanent houses

Encourage the students to design a permanent shelter for at least one of the organisms that lives in one of the habitats you have studied. The students could produce a sign for each habitat, explaining what lives there and warning people to be careful when walking through the area.

Presentation

Ask students to work in groups to prepare a PowerPoint presentation that explains why we must save the environment and the habitats that plants and animals live in. They should say that if we don't, they may well die.

At home

Ask students to make a list of all the times they have turned off lights, the air-conditioning or running water, or reused something. They should also say how their efforts will help the environment.

Plenary

Discuss with the students what sorts of damage humans do to the environment. Think of roads, rubbish tips, oil spills in the sea, etc. *What effect do we have on the wildlife?* One example is the Dodo, which is extinct due to over-hunting, the introduction of rats to its island and the destruction of its habitat.

47

Unit 2: Living things in their environment – Our environment

The objectives for this lesson are that students should be able to:

- Understand that they need to protect natural habitats and their environment

- Recognize ways that human activity affects the environment

- Learn how to reduce, re-use and recycle to protect their environment

- Make their own recycled paper.

SB pp.30–31 — *Starter*

- Come into the classroom with a water bottle (covered so students cannot see the contents).

- Tell the students you have been on a lovely walk recently and are looking forward to drinking the water you collected from a local stream.

- Pour out a glass of water revealing a filthy polluted drink that you have previously created by adding soil and bits of rubbish to the water.

- Your students should voice their horror at this – you don't drink the water but enquire of the students what the problem is. *This is fresh river water – it couldn't be more natural – could it?*

Explain

Problem pollution

Wherever we live on Earth we are close to other plants and animals. We need to share our planet but sometimes, in making our lives easier, we harm the places we should be caring about. As waste products from factories and towns are created, we have to put them somewhere and sometimes we carelessly throw them away, which leads to pollution and damages the habitats of other creatures.

What other sorts of pollution can the students think of? Look at the photographs on page 30 and discuss how human activity can lead to water, sea and air pollution, e.g. oil spills that can be very damaging to sea birds and marine life in general.

Dirty water

The water in your bottle is dirty because of unclean waste that has been dumped into the river. Not only does the water look dirty but there are possibly harmful things dissolved in the water that we can't see.

Sometimes oil refineries, factories and power stations use cold water to get rid of heat created by the industrial processes. The resulting hot water is discharged into rivers. This water isn't particularly dirty but the heat reduces the oxygen levels in the river and can cause the river life to die.

Cleaning up

When farmers use fertilizers on their crops, some of the chemicals can wash down into the water supply. When this happens or when sewage pollutes the water, small microscopic algae in the water grow very fast and the water becomes uninhabitable for other life.

Things to do

Reduce, re-use, recycle

Introduce the students to the ideas of reducing the amount of resources we use every day, not throwing things away after only using them once (e.g. using a lunch box that can be washed and re-used rather than packing lunch in foil or paper each day) and collecting waste for recycling into new objects, e.g. glass bottles and metal cans.

> ⚠ Safety first! Don't go through bins for examples of things that have been thrown away but could be re-used; this is unhygienic and possibly hazardous.

Encourage the students to make a list of everyday objects that they could reduce their use of (cars, electricity, packaging for food, etc.) What would they do instead? E.g. walk instead of getting the bus or car, reduce the amount of time they spend watching TV, turn the heating or air-conditioning down slightly to save power, choose food that is not over packaged, etc. Do the same for re-using and recycling.

Record

Students can make a poster about reducing consumption, re-using what they have and recycling things that have come to the end of their useful life.

Support

Focus on one thing such as saving water and find as many ways of saving or recycling water as you can, e.g. fixing dripping taps, washing the car less, etc.

Extend

Set up a compost heap to recycle food waste from lunch times (only raw food such as vegetable peelings and fruit, not cooked waste). Use homemade compost to enrich the soil in a school vegetable garden and eat the vegetables produced.

I wonder...

This provides an opportunity to mount a whole school campaign on reducing waste or just a personal promise to be more careful about the things we discard and dispose of without thinking.

Dig deeper

These questions are designed to raise awareness of how much we waste in our daily lives and how much of our household waste can be reduced, re-used or recycled. Focus too on waste energy as well as waste 'things'. We can reduce our energy consumption with relatively small changes which over the course of a year add to up to quite a lot.

More able students may wish to research the use of renewable energy such as wind, wave and solar energy.

Did you know?

These facts illustrate water wastage and ways of recycling materials.

- Water consumption differs from country to country. America has high usage per head of population whereas in Kenya the average person uses around 86 000 litres each year. Industry is a big consumer of water too – it takes 30 000

litres of water to make a car! We can reduce our individual consumption in a number of ways such as taking showers rather than baths, only using a washing machine when it has a full load, using a bowl of water to wash with rather than leaving a tap running and so on.

- Glass can be almost endlessly recycled, so too can metals. Paper on the other hand can be recycled about eight times; after that the fibres are too broken down to be used as paper again.

Other ideas

Making paper

Ask students to use waste paper to make recycled paper by making a paper 'soup'. Mix old paper with water and liquidize it to slurry, then spread it out on fine netting frames. Press out excess water and leave your paper to dry in the frames. Ironing the new paper will give it a smoother finish.

If you are near a recycling bank or plant you could use this as an opportunity to visit and to see the system of recycling in action.

At home
WS 21

Ask the students to think more about what they can re-use or recycle at home.

Ask students to complete WS 21 as homework.

Plenary

Use the plenary session to re-cap on the ideas and achievements or promises of the class to reduce, re-use and recycle resources in school and at home. Put up reminder signs to save water near taps and fountains, turn electrical equipment off rather than leaving it on standby. Investigate buying recycled paper products.

Unit 2: Living things in their environment – Unit 2 Review

The objectives for this lesson are that students should be able to:

- Check what they have learned about living things and their environment in this Unit

- Find out how they are working towards, within and beyond the Grade 4 level.

SB p.32   *Expectations*

Students working towards Grade 4 level will:

- Identify some local habitats

- Name a few of the organisms that live there and, with help, identify these using simple keys

- Make observations of animals and plants.

In addition, students working within Grade 4 level will:

- Identify some local habitats

- Name some of the organisms that live there

- Recognize that animals and plants are suited to their habitats

- State the food source of some animals

- Distinguish between those which eat plants and those which eat other animals

- Recognize that we need to protect animal and plant habitats

- Use simple keys to identify organisms

- Plan how to investigate some of the preferences of small animals found in the habitat

- Explain what was discovered

- Choose apparatus and decide how to use it.

Further to this, students working beyond Grade 4 level will also:

- Represent feeding relationships within a habitat by food chains

- Explain that food chains begin with a green plant which 'produces' food for other organisms

- Explain why it is necessary to use a reasonably large sample when investigating the preferences of small invertebrates.

Check-up

Discuss the picnic idea with the students. They should be able to answer the three tasks easily.

- Class 4 should not leave any rubbish about and not trample all over the ground

- Students should be able to show how to collect organisms in pitfall traps, pooters or by tree-beating.

Assessment   WS 22

Use the Unit 2 assessment on WS 22 to check the students' understanding of the content of the Unit. The answers are given opposite.

Name: _____ Date: _____

WS 22   Unit 2 assessment

1 Where might you find a fish living?
_____

2 What part of their body do these animals use to push themselves through water?
a) Duck _____
b) Salmon _____

3 Put some of these into a food chain.
Sun   algae   water   salmon   otter   (green plants)   insect
a) Which is the producer in this food chain? _____
b) Which are the consumers? _____
c) Which are the predators? _____

4 Add three questions to this key so that it correctly identifies the insects.

- Question a) _____
  - Yes
    - Question b) _____
      - Yes → **Ant**
      - No → **Spider**
  - No
    - Question c) _____
      - Yes → **Snail**
      - No → **Earthworm**

22   Heinemann Explore Science Grade 4

Answers

1 In the sea, a river or any other water

2 a A duck uses its feet.

   b A salmon uses its tail.

3 a The algae (green plants) are the producers.

   b The water insect, salmon and otter are the consumers.

   c The salmon and otter are the predators.

4 Check that the key works correctly.

   One example is:

   a Does it have legs?

   b Does it have 6 legs (or 8 legs)?

   c Does it have a shell?

The answer!

Refer back to the original question about the countryside. Piles of sticks and logs provide a place for small animals to live. Leaving grass longer encourages butterflies and other insects. Wild flowers are best suited to growing in long grass, as they would in nature.

And finally...

Set up a habitat for snails, worms or other small invertebrates for other classes to see. Consider buying an ant or worm farm. Set up a gerbil cage or fish tank, checking with the students what conditions they think will be needed. Always buy animals from a reputable dealer or supplier.

Unit 3: Keeping warm

The objectives for this Unit are that students should be able to:

- Discover how states of matter can be changed

- Find out how temperature can be measured using a thermometer

- Learn that some materials conduct heat and some insulate heat

- Take accurate measurements with a ruler.

SB p.33 Science background

Many students will talk about 'heat' rather than 'temperature'. Heat is a type of energy that can be transferred from one place to another. It can travel by radiation (without air), e.g. from the Sun to the Earth, by conduction (through metals) and by convection (through the movement of liquids and gases). This is more information than the students need, but will help you to use the correct language, i.e. heat moves or is conducted. We measure the temperature to say how hot or cold something is, not how much heat there is in it. Temperature is a measure of how hot or how cold something is. It is measured in degrees, with a thermometer.

It is important that students learn how to use thermometers correctly and safely. Learning to read a thermometer and its scale is a valuable skill. At this stage the thermometers should have the simplest scale possible, building up to finer divisions. Digital thermometers are easier to read, but are not as common as analogue. Learning to read the divisions of analogue scales is important for measuring with other instruments too.

Never use very hot or boiling water. Never put the students in danger of being scalded. Ice straight from the freezer will cause burns (freezer burns) as well as other damage. Skin can stick to ice so that when you remove your hand, the skin is stripped off. Leave ice to melt slightly so that it will have a layer of water on the surface, and it will be safe to handle.

Language

Celsius	Temperature scale, named after Anders Celsius, where 0 is the freezing point of pure water and 100 the boiling point of pure water.
Degrees	Unit of measurement of temperature.
Electricity	A flow of electrons that carry a negative charge, which is transferred into useful energy like light and heat. Students only need to know that electricity is a type of energy.
Heat	A type of energy that can move from place to place with or without a material to conduct it.
Temperature	How hot or cold something is.
Thermal	Related to heat.
Thermal conductor	Allows heat or electricity to pass through it easily.
Thermal insulator	Prevents or slows the movement of heat or electricity from one place to another.
Thermometer	An instrument used to measure how hot or cold something is, in degrees Celsius or Fahrenheit (apart from in the USA, Fahrenheit is rarely used).

The Words to learn list on page 33 of the *Student Book* can be used to make a classroom display.

Resources

- *Keeping Warm* Reader

- A range of thermometers, filled with red, blue or green coloured liquid, never poisonous mercury (silver in colour). Also, a fever strip thermometer. They should read to an accuracy of 1°

- ICT temperature sensor, either linked to a computer or hand-held

- Containers for water, e.g. china cups, plastic cups, polystyrene cups, glasses, metal beakers, etc.

- Glass beakers

- A range of materials, e.g. fabrics, paper, cardboard, cotton wool, polystyrene packaging material, bubble wrap, foil, etc.

- A range of spoons made of different materials, e.g. wood, plastic, metal, etc.

- Washing-up or mixing bowls

- Butter

- Some ice.

Bright ideas

- Using a digital microscope to study fabric structure can show that fabrics with lots of trapped air are good insulators. Expanded polystyrene, which is often used for packaging, contains pockets of air.

Knowledge check

Students will be aware that they can feel hot or cold and that ice lollies melt as they eat them. They will have noticed that lollies begin to melt as soon as they come out of the freezer.

- All students should have experienced putting on more clothes on a cool evening.

- They may not have experienced 'temperature' except as numbers on the weather forecast.

Skills check

Students need to:

- measure length accurately

- make observations and comparisons

- use appropriate vocabulary.

Some students will:

- recognize metals are good thermal, as well as electrical, conductors

- recognize that objects cool or warm up to room temperature.

Links to other subjects

Literacy:	Reading and following simple instructions, e.g. carrying out both the insulation activities
Numeracy:	Reading scales, e.g. thermometers. Organizing and interpreting simple data in bar graphs or line graphs
ICT:	Using a temperature sensor. Using a multimedia package to combine text and graphics to make a presentation. Using a digital microscope to study fabrics
History:	Finding out how thermometers were invented and who invented them

Let's find out...

The Unit opens with this question:

Not all countries are hot. In cold countries the loft can be the hottest part of the house. That's because heat rises. Heat can escape through the roof and the house will get cold. A layer of soft, fluffy material is put in the loft to keep the house warm. This material is called loft insulation. What would be a good material to slow down the escape of heat? Will a house in a cold country get warm if there is no heating?

Discuss the question. As the topic progresses, students will have the opportunity to experiment with materials and discover which is the best thermal insulator.

Unit 3: Keeping warm – Feeling hot

The objectives for this lesson are that students should be able to:

- Understand that temperature is a measure of how hot or cold things are

- Find out how thermometers are used to measure temperature

- Make a presentation about temperature using ICT

- Understand that our senses can feel temperature, but they are not accurate thermometers.

SB pp.34–35

Starter

- If you have a hand warmer, like those used by walkers, pass it around the class and ask the students to feel it. Follow this with an ice cube that has just started to melt. From this, the students should realize that we judge heat with our sense of touch.

- Show the students a picture of a hot furnace. Ask the students about heat; about hot places. *Where is this? How do we know this is a hot place? What might you do to stay cool? How do we measure temperature? What tool or instrument tells us accurately how warm or cold we are?*

Explain

Sense of...

Recap our five senses, asking students to point to the part of their body that does the sensing. Put out some objects and ask the students how they recognize them, e.g. oranges by smell, metals by their coldness, etc. Place a lit candle on a desk. How do you know that it is hot? Some students will put their hands close to it. Agree that it is touch that registers hot and cold.

> ⚠️ Use tealights, as they contain the hot wax. Make sure students don't place their hands above the flame, as heat rises. They will get burnt if they put their hand as close above the flame as they would the sides.

Feeling hot

Use a fever strip thermometer to take the temperature of one of the students to show how to measure normal body temperature. If possible, show some of the other types of thermometer used for taking body temperature, e.g. a clinical alcohol thermometer and an ear thermometer.

Things to do

Heat sense

Take three washing-up or mixing bowls and half fill each one with water of a different temperature. One of the bowls should have ice in it, one should have water that has been left to reach room temperature for a couple of hours and one should have warm water from the tap. Let the students put their hands first into the water at room temperature and then straight into one of the other two bowls. They can obviously feel the difference but how do they describe it?

Set up two bowls of water that have slightly different temperatures (use a thermometer to check first) and ask the students to say which is hotter. This will be almost impossible as our sense of touch is not accurate enough. They could try using their elbows where the skin is thin. Tell them that parents of young babies often use the 'elbow dip' to take the temperature of the baby's bathwater.

Record

The students could draw pictures of their hands and the bowls, describing how they used their sense of touch to tell which water was hottest. The pictures could be put up as a class display or used in a presentation.

Support

Place the bowls on paper towels on table tops and make sure that only one student at a time uses them to avoid knocking them over. There is no need to dry hands between tests. Some students will have difficulty in describing how the water felt. Encourage them to use words like 'tingling' and 'numb' as well as hotter and colder.

Extend

From the first set of bowls, all students should be able to say which bowl of water was hottest.

By the law of averages, 50% of the students will correctly say which bowl of the two warm waters was warmer, but this will be purely a guess!

Some students could try the 'trick' in the 'Other ideas' section below.

I wonder...

Mercury is not used for thermometers because it, and its fumes, are poisonous. A harmless coloured liquid is used instead.

Dig deeper

The forehead thermometers that change colour with temperature are not very accurate, but they do give an instant reading and a general idea of the person's body temperature.

Did you know?

The clinical, or medical, thermometer was invented by a doctor, Sir Thomas Allbutt. Before this, it took 20 minutes and a thermometer 30 cm long to take a person's temperature!

Other ideas

Temperature trick

Show the students how to trick your senses to feel something different! In turn, let them place one hand in cold water and the other in warm. Then they place both hands into the same bowl of lukewarm water. *How does it feel? Which hand feels hotter? Why?*

The 'trick' shows that our sense of touch works by comparison. This is why water in a swimming pool feels warm if you have a cold shower first.

Some students will be able to say why the hand that has been in the cold water rather than the warm water finds the water hotter, i.e. the hand registers a greater temperature change. Our sense of touch is good for big changes in temperature but not for small ones.

Presentation

Ask the students to use word processing software to write about ways that you can detect heat or cold. They could include their senses and say why they think this is not very accurate. They could use each other to point out their senses and prepare a demonstration of the activity they did. Or they could explain why the swimming pool feels warm after a cold shower and cold after a warm shower.

At home

Ask the students to find out the body temperature of someone who is ill. Generally, this can be between 38°C and 40°C, or 101°F and 104°F.

Plenary

Try a quick word association game or mind map. Write the word 'temperature' on the board and ask the students to give all the words they can that are associated with it. Then link the words together, as below.

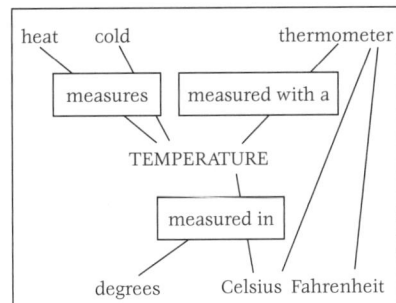

Unit 3: Keeping warm – Measuring temperature

The objectives for this lesson are that students should be able to:

- Find out that there are lots of different thermometers

- Learn how to take accurate readings from a thermometer

- Discover that objects gain or lose heat until they reach room temperature

- Take the temperature of their classroom.

SB pp.36–37

Starter

- Take into the class, carefully, a cup of coffee or tea that is too hot to drink. Talk about being very thirsty but say that your drink is too hot. *What should I do so that I can drink it quickly?* Some students may suggest blowing on it, others may suggest leaving it for a while. Ask the students what will happen if you leave the drink on your desk. Most should tell you that it will 'cool down'.

- Alternatively, come in complaining that you haven't had time for your porridge this morning, so you have brought it with you! Take a spoonful and pull a face. It's too cold! *Why has it become cold?* Tell the students that you made it with hot milk this morning.

- Ask the students how hot things can be cooled down – by blowing, adding ice or cold water, for example.

Explain

How hot?

The students will need to know how to read the scale on the thermometer. The three illustrations in the *Student Book* are examples of thermometers at 50, 65 and 90°C. Give the students practice reading ruler scales, explaining that they are similar to thermometers, or use a thermometer to find out what temperature the room is.

Show a range of thermometers, including soil, forehead (strips), clinical, and room thermometers. If you have access to digital ones and any old-fashioned instruments, even as pictures, use them too.

The first thermometers were filled with air and developed by Hero over 2000 years ago. In about 1600 Galileo and Santorio first calibrated thermometers.

The word comes from the Greek 'therme' meaning heat and the Latin 'metrum' meaning to measure.

Room temperature

It is important to remember that heat travels not cold. It travels from hot things and to cold ones until everything in one place is at the same temperature (except things that make their own heat, like a fire or your body). We call this room or ambient temperature.

Cold is the absence of heat energy. Closing the door does not keep the cold out, it keeps the heat in (although draughts – moving air – can whistle in to replace the lost heat).

Things to do

Final temperature

Students will need at least five beakers per group or pair. They will need to half fill each of them with water of different temperatures. Do not use water hotter than the hot tap. The cold water could have an ice cube in it. Some students may notice that the water level increases as the ice melts. Alternatively, place the water in the fridge for an hour before using it.

Teach the students the correct way to use a thermometer. It must be kept upright, so that the scale is level with the liquid inside. The bulb needs to be kept in the liquid, otherwise it will quickly move towards room temperature. The beaker must be left on the desk and the students should bend down to read the scale, rather than lifting the beaker, or the thermometer, to their eye. For safety reasons, liquids are not normally stirred with a thermometer as the thermometer could break.

Record

The students can record the temperatures in a table and then plot them in a bar chart.

Support

While the students are waiting for the water to reach room temperature, give them some practice at reading thermometers.

Extend

Some may suggest taking the temperature every 30 minutes or at least taking timed readings to observe the way in which the water changes temperature. These can be plotted into a line graph. This could also be extended into an enquiry. The temperatures could be taken with a digital thermometer or a sensor linked to a computer, which will produce a line graph for the students to interpret.

I wonder...

Each beaker of water should reach the same temperature, but it will be the temperature in the fridge, not room temperature. You could set this up and leave it until next lesson to check, if necessary.

Biographies

Fahrenheit was the inventor of the modern thermometer. He gave us the Fahrenheit scale: 32°F being the freezing point of water and 212°F being its boiling point. (Anders Celsius later devised the Centigrade or Celsius scale, which is metric.)

Did you know?

Different people use a range of units to measure temperature. The kelvin used by scientists doesn't use degrees. 'Absolute zero' is its zero point. This is the temperature at which all atoms stop moving. It is a theoretical temperature, as it has not been reached – yet!

Other ideas

Highs and lows

Ask the students to hold a thermometer firmly, but safely, in their hands. *Can you explain what has happened?* What temperature did they read? Now let them put the thermometer under cold running water. *What do you notice about the coloured liquid in the thermometer? What temperature does it read now?*

Presentation

Ask the students to prepare a presentation about what happens to a hot dinner and an ice cream left in a room for a while, and to explain what happens. This is harder than it looks as the students will probably assume that the dinner's heat is lost to the room and that the ice cream's cold is also lost! Remind them that cold cannot travel. However, the heat from the hot dinner can travel and warm up the ice cream. Eventually, both will be at room temperature.

At home

WS
23

Ask students to complete WS 23 as homework.

Plenary

Show the students some objects at different temperatures and ask them what will happen to them. *What temperature will they all eventually reach?*

Unit 3: Keeping warm – Hot and cold places

The objectives for this lesson are that students should be able to:

- Understand that different countries are at different temperatures and why this is

- Understand that different places in the same room can be at different temperatures

- Draw a temperature map of their classroom and test their predictions of the hottest and coldest parts

- Learn that 20°C is a comfortable room temperature.

SB
pp.38–39

Starter

- Enter the classroom saying you are cold. Sit by the air-conditioning or an open door and still complain about being cold. *Where should I sit if I am cold? Why? What is it about the place you have chosen that will make me less cold?*

- Refer back to the Unit on growing plants. *Where should we put a plant to grow well? It is not only light that they need, but what else?* Obviously they need warmth. *Where would they grow best?*

- Ask the students what happens at different temperatures. *At what temperature does water freeze? At what temperature does a human feel comfortable?*

Explain

Hot or not?

On the board or using an OHP, draw a weather map of your country with some weather symbols and do a presentation about the weather. The students will know that the hotter places are going to be where the Sun symbols are. Discuss what temperatures they would expect to see.

Keeping your cool

The plan of the kitchen is a forerunner to the Hot spots activity. The students should realize that the fizzy drink should be kept in the fridge, as it becomes fizzier when left in warmer air. Most students will have experienced this. The students should also recall that plant seedlings will need

to be put somewhere warm to grow well. The ice lolly should go in the freezer, otherwise it will melt, unless it is eaten first!

Things to do

WS
24

Hot spots

The students will need to set up thermometers in various places around the classroom. Remind them to place them carefully so that they cannot be knocked over or roll off surfaces. An elastic band twisted round the end of a thermometer prevents it from rolling. Ensure that the students do not put the thermometers inside anything as this will affect the readings. They could set up the thermometers first thing in the morning and then read them every hour during the day. Alternatively, they could set them up during the lesson, take readings until the end of school and continue the next morning until 24 hours are up. Although the areas of the classroom should only have a slight variation in temperature from each other, there should be a greater variation at certain times of the day. This activity could be done with a temperature sensor and a computer.

The students should plan what to do and the type of thermometer to use, based on the ones they have already seen. The readings should show that some places are warmer than others and that room temperature changes during the day.

Record

The students can record the classroom temperatures on WS 24. These results can then be presented as a graph, showing the coldest and warmest places in the room or, using one thermometer, how the temperature changes through the day. This can be quite complicated. Ask groups of students to plot the graph for a particular area, rather than asking all the students to plot all of them on the same graph. The readings can be plotted as a bar chart or a line graph. If this is done on the computer and projected onto a screen, the whole class results can be overlaid, so that you can see which is the warmest area.

Support

Prepare a plan of the classroom and photocopy it. Include where the windows are, the air-conditioning outlets and any doors or windows that are usually open.

Extend

All students should notice that some areas of the classroom are warmer than others. Some will notice that the areas closest to a heat source, e.g. a sunny window, will be warmer.

Let the students use different thermometers to see if they read the same each temperature, or use two of the same kind of thermometer and duplicate their readings. They may be able to explain why this is more accurate.

I wonder...

The students should realize that any other classroom will be a similar temperature and will also have the same sorts of variation in temperature, depending on its air-conditioning outlets and windows. Ask them what you could do if the Sun was very hot.

Dig deeper

Some materials are thermal conductors and some are thermal insulators. Recap the meanings of insulate and conduct; the students will need them in the next lesson.

Did you know?

These facts show that people go to some trouble to keep their homes at a constant temperature of about 20°C. All cars also have heaters and some have air-conditioning units for our comfort.

Other ideas

Digital use

Obviously the best way to see the fluctuations in temperature over a 24-hour period is to record the temperature regularly during that period. However, you probably don't stay at school that long. Using a computer-linked digital thermometer that can take a sample temperature every hour would be ideal. Unless you have several, you might have to set it up in a different place each day to record the temperature in the areas indicated by the students. Use a computer to draw graphs of the temperatures.

Weather station

Encourage the students to set up their own weather station with a rainfall gauge and a maximum/minimum thermometer. They could also explore the difference between a thermometer kept in the shade and one left in the sunshine.

Presentation

The students could produce a large version of WS 24 to display, showing the hot and cold places, or average room temperature for the day.

At home

WS 25

Ask the students to look at the temperature range of the oven and the fridge in their kitchen. What temperature is the freezer?

Ask students to complete WS 25 as homework.

Plenary

Ask the students to produce an acrostic of a word linked to heat, temperature, thermometer, etc. to show what they have learned so far. For instance:

Does

Everything

Get to

Room temperature

Eventually

Even

Soup?

59

Unit 3: Keeping warm – Keeping cool

The objectives for this lesson are that students should be able to:

- Use a thermometer carefully and accurately

- Understand that they must handle a thermometer with care

- Find out about insulation and how it works

- Draw a suitable graph to display the results of their investigations.

SB pp.40–41   *Starter*

- Take a melting ice lolly into the classroom. Ask the students what you should do with it, as you have to teach and can't eat it until later. Tell them the freezer has broken down.

- Give each student or group of students an ice cube (not straight from the freezer) to pass around. Ask them where they would put it to stop it melting. They should realize that keeping it in their hands causes it to melt, as their hands are warm.

- Discuss what students have seen melting and distinguish melting from other types of change.

The challenge

Read the speech bubbles on page 40 in the *Student Book*. Discuss the problem that Farida has. Which do they think is the best way to stop her ice lollies from melting? The students also need to think about how to measure whether the ice has melted or not.

What to do   WS 26

Ask the students why there is a suggestion of wrapping up the ice lollies. What are they trying to prevent? Ask them how ice melts in the first place. The ice is heating up, but they may think it is because the cold is escaping from the ice. Remind them that cold does not travel and to think in terms of trying to keep the heat out or away from the ice instead.

The students will need an ice lolly and thermometer for each type of insulation they want

to test. Freeze the ice lollies for about 24 hours before you need them.

The students may expect that the temperature of the ice will be 0 °C. Remind them that the ice is already starting to melt as it is out of the freezer and the temperature will be above freezing. Asking them what they expect to happen eventually should remind them that the ice will get to room temperature after a few hours.

Suggest that they make their final investigation of the insulated ice lollies when one with no insulation reaches room temperature.

Before starting the investigation, students can use the top table on WS 26 to predict how long each ice lolly will be after the investigation.

What you need

- Ice lollies

- Thermometers, including digital examples

- Various insulating materials, e.g. fabric, paper, cardboard, cotton wool, straw, packaging materials such as polystyrene

- Stopwatches

- This will be messy work unless you wrap each ice lolly in cling film at the start. Alternatively, you could use wrapped ice pops.

What to check

To make this test fair, the students must make sure that all the frozen ice lollies are the same size initially. Farida was measuring the length of her lollies. Your students could do this and discuss how accurate this would be.

Ask the students to work in groups with each group carrying out one investigation using one type of material. The students can then pool their results later. This is especially useful if the students have decided to take the temperature every five minutes or so (see Extend).

The starting temperature is unimportant, except that it is below room temperature.

Support

If you have one, use a computer-linked temperature sensor in one of the beakers so that the students can check their readings as they go.

Extend

All students should be able to recognize that the ice will melt if left on its own. Some will realize that by insulating the ice it will melt more slowly.

To investigate this, the students could record the temperature at the start and at the end of the lesson, seeing which ice lolly had warmed up the most. The problem with this is that they may all have warmed up and a conclusion might be difficult. Taking the temperature every five minutes will enable the students to see which ice lolly is warming up the fastest.

What did you find?

Record

The students should use WS 26 to record the actual length of each ice lolly. This data should produce a bar chart.

The students can convert their recorded data into a graph. As a fallback, they could use the idealized data given in the *Student Book*. The data in this enquiry is not continuous so only a bar graph, consistent with the data, can be produced.

Present

Ask students to present their findings in groups, perhaps using ICT. If the students made video clips of the ice lolly melting, encourage them to import these to show what happens. If they record an insulated ice lolly melting next to one left in room temperature, they can easily show the relative rate of melting. They should also include their table of results and a chart or graph.

Can you do better?   WS 27

Show the students the report on WS 27 and read it together. It is a good report and Farida has thought carefully about which materials to use and why. She also concluded which material kept the lolly cold for longest. Perhaps she should have measured the length of the lolly as soon as she took it out of the freezer. This would give her an idea of whether any of the methods of insulation was good enough to use again, i.e. it would make it relative.

Now predict

By wrapping more layers of newspaper around the ice lolly it should stay colder longer. The paper traps layers of air and air is a good insulator.

Other ideas

Lolly cool box

Let the students investigate whether the insulation needs to be all the way round the ice lolly or just at the top and bottom. *Do ice cubes melt faster in a disposable cup with a lid on, or without?* Use this example to challenge the idea about 'cold coming in'.

The thicker the better

Set a similar challenge to the box/container idea, but using one type of insulation, e.g. paper. The students should vary the thickness or number of layers used.

ICT ideas

If you have a computer-linked temperature sensor, the students could set it up to do the sampling for them, with different types of insulation.

At home

Ask the students to investigate the types of packaging that are used to keep things cold. *Why do supermarkets sell padded freezer bags?*

Plenary

Show the students a supermarket freezer bag or a sleeping bag. *Why is this a good thermal insulator?*

Ask them to draw and label a diagram of their activity, explaining how the insulation worked. Check that they understand that it stopped the heat from getting in, rather than the cold getting out.

61

Unit 3: Keeping warm – Investigating insulators

The objectives for this lesson are that students should be able to:

- Understand how insulation helps keep things warm

- Investigate how to keep liquid hot for a long time

- Explain what they thought would happen and what they found out

- Evaluate how fair the walkers' test was.

SB pp.42–43 — Starter

- Say you are cold and that you need to put on another jumper. Ask the students why. They may say it is to 'get warm'. The jumper doesn't actually make you warmer; it keeps the heat from leaving your body so quickly, so you feel warmer.

- Wear some walking gear, complete with a rucksack full of drinks containers and items/fabrics to test for insulation. Ask the students to feel the outside of a vacuum flask of tea to show it's not hot. Show them that the liquid inside is hot.

- Empty the contents of the rucksack onto your desk. Ask the students to use whatever they can find to try and keep the tea warm as the flask will not hold enough for everyone.

The challenge

Read the opening of page 42 in the *Student Book*. Discuss the problem with the students. They must find the best way of keeping tea warm. This means reducing the amount of heat escaping into the room.

What to do

The walkers have limited themselves to the objects they would normally have in their backpacks. The liquid in the containers needs to be measured and the temperature taken. If this is just taken at the end of the investigation, you have to guarantee the start temperature is the same. By measuring the temperature change over time, the start temperature is less important. Use water from the same jug or tap.

⚠ Boiling water must NOT be used. Use water from a hot water tap. This should be regulated at a safe temperature in schools.

What you need

- Thermometers, including computer-linked temperature sensor if possible

- Different containers

- Small items of clothing to test for insulation

- A rucksack

- Stopwatches

- Measuring cylinders or jugs

- Warm tap water.

What to check

Measure the amount of water to ensure the test is fair. If the students change the insulating material, they must keep the material the cup is made from the same.

⚠ Make sure that the water stays in the beakers. Spills cause accidents!

Support

Some students may need help in recording the temperature. If they get bored with having to wait 40 minutes, set this up just before lunch and then measure the temperature afterwards.

Extend

All students should be able to recognize which method kept the tea hottest the longest.

Some students could take the temperature every five minutes, and draw and interpret a line graph.

What did you find? — WS 28 | WS 29

If they are taking the temperature difference after 40 minutes students should use WS 28, but if they are taking it every five minutes then they should use WS 29.

Record

If the students recorded the temperature change in each container after 40 minutes, the graph will be a bar chart as the data is not continuous. If they recorded the fall in temperature every five minutes, then the graph will be a line graph as the data ican be seen as continuous.

As a fallback, they could use the walkers' idealized data given in the *Student Book*. The data in this enquiry is not continuous so only a bar graph can be generated on WS 28.

Present

Ask the students to look at the chart or graph and 'tell its story'. Encourage them to write what they did and what happened, including drawing the table of results and chart. Let each group of students present their findings perhaps using PowerPoint. The students could also make a class display on insulation using their data.

Can you do better?

Students might argue that they need to keep the test fairer, by using the same container and wrapping it in different insulation. While two different containers were tested, both containers had a lid and were wrapped in the same materials.

Now predict

Wrapping the container in bubble wrap is one effective way of demonstrating the importance of air as an insulator. Wrapping in cling film – effectively bubble wrap without the bubbles – is not so effective.

Many people warm up the inside of a vacuum flask with hot water before using it. The students could do a test run with a container to see if this makes a difference, using one that has been warmed and one that hasn't.

Other ideas

Heat on the outside

Try and obtain thermometer strips that are similar to those used on the forehead. They can be wrapped around the outside of a layer of insulation to measure the temperature. They show how much heat is escaping through the insulation. The better the insulation, the lower the temperature. Some suppliers produce cups with strip thermometers incorporated.

ICT ideas

If you have one, use a temperature sensor on the computer to record the fall in temperature in any or all of the insulation types.

Students can use a digital microscope or hand lenses to look at the fibre and the holes in the various types of material and make a prediction about how good an insulator each would be.

At home

Ask the students to look around their home for examples of thermal insulators, e.g. oven gloves, saucepan handles, place mats and clothes.

Plenary

Discuss the clothes students might wear for changing weather and climate conditions – or for visits to other parts of the world. Challenge the commonly held view that some clothes are themselves 'warm'. They are good insulators that retain body heat.

Unit 3: Keeping warm – Conducting heat

The objectives for this lesson are that students should be able to:

- Understand that metals are not good insulators as they conduct heat

- Find out that a vacuum flask is a good insulator

- Discover that good thermal conductors are also good electrical conductors

- Make a list of insulators of food, people and their school or homes.

SB pp.44–45 — *Starter*

- Split the class into three groups. Tell them that one group represents the liquid, one is the insulation and one is the air outside. Give the liquid group four red card squares each. These represent heat. The air doesn't have any cards. Explain that it would be fairer if the heat were evenly spread out between the liquid and the air (this is how an object reaches room temperature). Start with only liquid and air. The liquid group, which is hot, starts passing the red cards to the air group, who are asking them to give them up. Continue until each student has two red cards.

- Return the 'heat' cards to the liquid group. Now put the insulation group between the liquid and the air. The insulation will prevent the liquid reaching the air easily. Some 'liquid' students will push past the insulation, or there may be gaps in the insulation, but the exchange of the heat, or in this case the red cards, will be much slower.

- Show the students a picture of a person in warm clothes. *Is it the clothes that are warm? Or do they keep in the person's body heat?*

Explain

Hot or cold?

This links back to properties of materials studied in Grade 3. An insulator slows the movement of heat.

Vacuum flasks

The vacuum flask has two walls. Between these walls there is a vacuum – no air. Heat cannot pass through a vacuum and so hot or cold food or drink

inside the flask cannot lose or gain heat. The lid and bottom attachment may still conduct heat and so the inside temperature will change – slowly.

Thermal underwear

Clothes similar to those worn by skiers have a waterproof outer layer, a layer of air, a thick layer of polyester wadding, another layer of air and finally an inner cotton lining for comfort. Husky dogs have a thick fur coat – but even the hairs are hollow and air-filled, adding to the insulation properties of the coat.

Things to do   WS 30

Runny honey

Use butter or honey. Both make a bit of a mess when they run off the spoon! Make sure you have some paper towels under the bowls of water and under the spoon handles.

The spoons will need to be placed in quite hot water, so this might be better done as a demonstration with the students, in groups, timing the different spoons.

The activity also asks the students to think about the materials for saucepans. The handle will need to be an insulator and the pan a conductor.

Record

Students should use WS 30 to record their results in the table. They can then use their results to draw a bar chart.

The students could draw a diagram of the equipment, with the results next to each spoon and a conclusion underneath.

Support

Agree the point at which to stop the timer. It can either be when the honey first drips off or when it has all run off.

Extend

All students should find that the honey on the metal spoons melts and goes runny fastest. This shows that metal conducts heat fastest.

Some students could try a range of metals to observe whether all metals conduct at the same speed. This links to why some saucepans are copper-bottomed (the copper conducts the heat evenly and well) and whether aluminium camping saucepans are good thermal conductors.

I wonder...

Good thermal insulators are good electrical insulators too. Fabrics, fibres and natural materials of all kinds both conserve heat and resist the flow of electricity. Metals are good conductors of electricity and they also conduct heat away from your hand quickly, which is why they feel cold to the touch. But good thermal conductors are not necessarily good electrical conductors – non-metallic materials can 'feel cold' but not conduct electricity well.

Dig deeper

Students should explore how internal energy which is greater in a hot object transfers to a cooler object which has less energy.

Did you know?

This shows that warm-blooded animals have body insulation.

Mammals and birds are warm-blooded – they maintain their body temperature. Other animals, including fish, reptiles, amphibians and all the invertebrates are cold-blooded – they are at the temperature of their surroundings. It takes a lot of energy to be warm-blooded, but your body doesn't slow down when the weather turns cold.

Other ideas

Hot rods

Set up some rods of different metals borrowed from a secondary school. At regular intervals, attach some drawing pins with candle wax. Support each rod so they are level. Set a tealight at one end and time how long it takes for all the drawing pins to fall off. Heat travels along the metal and the drawing pins fall off one by one as the wax melts.

Presentation

Let the students present the game in the starter activity to another class, or in an assembly, to show other students that heat is transferred and how insulation slows its movement.

At home

WS 31

Ask the students to spot the insulator. Let them compile a list of clothes and food containers and bring it to school.

Ask students to complete WS 31 as homework.

Plenary

Ask the students to draw a cartoon showing what happens to a material that is insulated. Include labels or speech bubbles to show what is happening.

Unit 3: Keeping warm – Unit 3 Review

The objectives for this lesson are that students should be able to:

- Check what they have learned about states of matter in this Unit

- Find out how they are working towards, within and beyond the Grade 4 level.

SB p.46 **Expectations**

Students working towards Grade 4 level will:

- Recognize that temperature is a measure of how hot or cold objects are

- Identify some everyday uses of thermal insulators

- Use thermometers to measure temperature

- Present results in tables prepared for them.

In addition, students working within Grade 4 level will:

- Identify some materials that are good thermal insulators and some everyday uses of these

- Recognize that the same materials that keep cold objects cold also keep warm objects warm

- Suggest how to investigate a question

- Construct tables for their results and offer simple explanations for results.

Further to this, students working beyond Grade 4 level will also:

- Recognize that objects cool or warm to the temperature of their surroundings when they are left

- Recognize that metals are both good thermal and good electrical conductors.

Check-up

Students could suggest places like the refrigerator for Maalik's sandwiches.

Assessment   WS 32

Use the Unit 3 assessment to check the students' understanding of the content of the Unit. The answers are given opposite.

Name: _____   Date: _____

WS 32 Unit 3 assessment

1 What is temperature a measure of? _____

2 Aditi and Ishaan were making a snack for tea. They each had a cup of tea and a bowl of ice cream. Their mother called them to the table to eat it, but they wanted to finish watching a cartoon.

   a) Write down the temperature you think their tea and the ice cream are. Don't forget the units.

   Tea _____   Ice cream _____

   b) Why weren't they very happy when they reached the table 10 minutes later?

   _____

   c) What temperature will tea become if it is left for 1 hour?

3 Write down the temperatures shown on these thermometers.

   0 10 20 30 40 50 60 70 80 90 100 ___°C

   0 10 20 30 40 50 60 70 80 90 100 ___°C

   0 10 20 30 40 50 60 70 80 90 100 ___°C

4 What can a thermometer be filled with? _____

32   Heinemann Explore Science Grade 4

Answers

1   Temperature measures how hot or how cold things are.

2   **a**   Tea = 70 to 100°C   Ice cream = 0°C

   b   They weren't very happy because their tea was cold and their ice cream had melted.

   c   Room temperature or around 20°C

3   50°C; 42°C; 85°C

4   A thermometer can be filled with mercury or liquid dye.

The answer!

Refer back to the original question about heating a home in a cold country. If you can get some cotton wool and some loft insulation for the students to see, this will illustrate how loose-textured it is and that it traps air. Use cotton wool as a material to insulate a cup of tea.

And finally...

Set up a display of a wide range of insulating materials and label them with their uses. This will show how people keep warm or cold and how they keep food warm or cold.

67

Unit 4: Separating solids and liquids

The objectives for this Unit are that students should be able to:

- Re-cap that there are three types of matter – solids, liquids and gases

- Find how matter can change from one state to another

- Explain the evidence they have gathered means

- Use evidence to predict things they don't yet know.

SB p.47 Science background

Whether a substance is a solid or a liquid depends upon how its particles are arranged. Particles in a solid are tightly packed and unmoving. In a liquid they are less regular and can move over one another; this enables a liquid to flow.

Although they are unmoving, particles of solids vibrate. When a solid is heated, the particles vibrate more quickly until, when the melting point of that material is reached, the links between them are broken and the solid melts. This happens at different temperatures for different materials. The reverse is true when a liquid freezes; the particles slow down and move closer together to form a regular pattern.

When a solid is added to water it may dissolve; i.e. it becomes thoroughly mixed in the liquid and is spread evenly throughout the solution. Students often say that a white solid has 'disappeared' in water rather than dissolved; they do not realize that the solid substance is still present.

One way we separate mixtures of materials is to use the physical properties of the materials. Different-sized solid particles can be separated by sieving, magnetic metals can be removed using a magnet and insoluble (undissolved) solids in a liquid can be separated using a filter. Solutions cannot be separated using a filter but evaporating the water can retrieve the solids.

The word 'material' is often used interchangeably with 'fabric'. Students should be encouraged to think of a fabric as being a type of cloth, whereas material can apply to a much wider range of substances.

Language

Dissolve	Where one substance mixes so completely in another that it is present throughout – usually where a solid is completely dispersed throughout a liquid
Evaporate	The change of water from liquid to water vapour that occurs above $0\,^\circ C$
Filter	To retrieve an insoluble solid from a liquid
Filter paper	A fine paper sieve which allows liquid to pass through but stops solids
Freeze	To change a liquid into a solid by cooling
Insoluble	Not able to dissolve
Liquid	A substance that can flow and takes the shape of its container
Melt	To change a solid into a liquid by heating
Particle	An atom or molecule or a very tiny amount
Sieve	To separate different-sized solid particles by passing them through a mesh or grid
Solid	A substance that keeps its shape and volume and is difficult to compress
Solidify	To turn a liquid into a solid
Soluble	Able to dissolve
Solution	A mixture of a soluble substance in water resulting in a transparent liquid (a solution may be transparent but coloured)
Suspension	Where particles are suspended in liquid and are neither entirely soluble or insoluble. Suspensions are cloudy because the suspended particles reflect and scatter light

The Words to learn list on page 47 of the *Student Book* can be used to make a classroom display.

Resources

- *Solids, Liquids and Gases* Reader
- A selection of safe soluble and insoluble solids, e.g. sugar, salt, flour, icing sugar, rice, instant coffee, non-bio washing powder, cornflour, soap, custard powder, jelly, butter, chocolate, dried pulses or pasta
- A selection of safe liquids, e.g. water, milk, cooking oil, liquid detergent, syrup, vinegar, honey, shampoo
- Hand lenses and magnifying glasses
- A selection of different-sized containers for liquids
- Spoons
- Measuring cylinders
- Transparent beakers
- Bowls
- Cupcake cases
- A selection of sieves
- Filter paper
- Funnels
- A seconds timer.

Bright ideas

- Clear tap water can sometimes be difficult for students to see easily. Add a few drops of food colouring to increase the visibility.

Knowledge check

- Everything in the world is made from particles of matter.
- Materials can be solid, liquid or gas.
- A solid has a definite shape.
- A liquid takes the shape of its container.
- Some solids behave like liquids, but poured solids do not make a flat surface.
- Some solids become liquids when they are heated. Some liquids become solids when they are cooled.
- When a liquid evaporates it becomes a gas.

- Water and ice are made of the same substance and can change from one to the other.
- Some solids have to be very hot before they change.
- Sieving can separate solids.
- Insoluble solids can be separated from a liquid by filtering.
- Filters cannot separate soluble solids in solutions.

> ⚠ Warn students never to taste any of the substances they are using unless you ask them to.

Skills check

Students need to:

- make careful observations and measurements
- collect evidence and decide how good it is
- use their evidence to explain what they found out.

Some students will:

- be able to explain that some materials, e.g. metals, need to be heated to very high temperatures before they melt
- explain that when solids dissolve they break up so small that they pass through the holes in filter paper.

Links to other subjects

Literacy: Chemistry features in many stories, e.g. Professor Snape the Potions master in the Harry Potter stories.

Let's find out...

The Unit opens with this question:

> *The river near Mansoor's school is polluted. Class 4 have cleared away all the rubbish they could find from the river and its banks. The water looks very clean and clear but fish still won't live in it. What can the problem be?*

Can we always tell what is in a liquid? Do you think there might be something in the river that we can't see?

69

Unit 4: Separating solids and liquids – Properties of materials

The objectives for this lesson are that students should be able to:

- Understand that solids, liquids and gases are all made up of particles

- Discover that the particles in solids, liquids and gases are arranged in different ways

- Measure the volume of liquids accurately

- Find out how heating and cooling materials can change their properties.

SB pp.48–49

Starter

Show the students a glass containing water. *What is in this glass? How do we know it is a liquid?* It pours, it fills the glass so that there are no spaces and it has a flat top. Add a drop of ink or food colour. The ink in the liquid will swirl through it and will soon colour it all.

Tell the students that they are going to find out more about the properties of liquids and of solids.

Explain

Atomic Greek

Explain that Democritus thought that if you kept cutting something in half you'd eventually obtain the smallest possible particle. He called this an atom, the Greek word for 'indivisible'. Atoms are the building blocks of the whole world – everything is made from them.

Shape up

Atoms are so small that we can't see them. They often join together to make bigger particles called molecules – these are invisible to the naked eye too.

Let the students pretend to be atoms or molecules in a solid. Invite them to link closely together in a square shape. Ask them to 'vibrate' or wiggle on the spot. This is what it's like to be a solid – tightly packed, regular shaped, but difficult to move.

Materials that are solids have their own shape and they are difficult to squash. Show the students salt or sugar crystals under a microscope. Although they are small, they have their own regular shape.

Get moving

Liquids are made of atoms and molecules too, but they're arranged more loosely than solids and can move around a bit more.

Let the students pretend to be the atoms or molecules of a liquid. They don't have to stand quite as close to their neighbours but they must still be joined. Ask them to move a little way backwards and forwards. They don't need to keep the same shape because the atoms or molecules can move apart and into other spaces.

Moving freely

The particles in a solid are locked in place. They may vibrate, but they stay just where they are. Sometimes they are in tidy patterns and sometimes they are randomly packed. You can demonstrate this. A crystal – whether it's a diamond or a sugar crystal – has these particles in a tidy lattice. A thin polystyrene cup has them in rows – try tearing one downwards into strips. A thick polystyrene cup has random particles and tears unevenly. Water has particles that pour, rolling over each other. Particles in gases are free to move and spread; you can smell perfume from a distance.

Things to do

Measure water

Ask the students to measure 100 ml of water in a measuring cylinder, then pour it into differently-shaped containers and notice how it behaves.

Record

Make a paper display of a large measuring cylinder and label the important features, e.g. 'the scale is measured in cm^3', 'the scale begins at the base', 'there is a wide base to stop it falling over', 'divisions come in groups of 2, 5, 10 or 100', etc.

Support

Remind students how to measure the volume of liquids. Explain how the top of the water curves down slightly; this is called the meniscus.

Extend

Play a game to guess the volume of a bottle. Collect several differently-shaped containers. *How much liquid can they hold?* Then let the students test their predictions. The closest guess wins.

I wonder...

Fill a plastic container with water so it's almost overflowing. Top it with a square of card. Put the jar in a freezer until the water turns to ice. Show the students that the ice has lifted the card above the top of the jar. If the water had no room for expansion, the jar would have cracked from the pressure.

Dig deeper

Waterwheels have used water to power machines for centuries. Now we use water from reservoirs or the sea to turn turbines and generate power.

Did you know?

Anyone who's been to a rock concert has probably seen 'dry ice' used on stage. This is carbon dioxide gas cooled to its solid state.

Other ideas

WS 33

Ice hand

A fun way to demonstrate that solids have shape and liquids do not is to make an ice hand and let it melt. Fill a latex glove with water, add food colouring and let it freeze. Place the glove in a deep tray in the classroom. As it melts the students will see that the solid shape is lost.

Mystery materials

Show some safe domestic materials to students – milk, sugar, salt, cooking oil, etc. Pour them into different containers and ask students to complete WS 33.

ICT ideas

If you have one, use a temperature sensor to record temperatures in and around a fridge. *How does the temperature of the freezer compare with the main part of the fridge? Is the fridge the same temperature throughout? How much cooler is the fridge than the air temperature outside it?* Let the students make a temperature map of a refrigerator.

Presentation

Ask the students to pretend that they are investigative reporters. They must find out if adding ice to drinks in cafés is a good deal for consumers or not. Get the students to work out the difference in volume of water used to fill an empty glass and one containing ice cubes. Let them present the results as a report, using ICT.

At home

Encourage the students to make a list of solids and liquids found in one room in their home – the kitchen and bathroom are good places to look. *Are there any materials that you're not sure about?*

Plenary

On the board, list some of the key words from the lesson. Using these key words, create a mind map or concept map, drawing arrows to join words and then writing joining words on the arrows, for example:

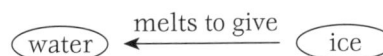

water ← melts to give ← ice

Unit 4: Separating solids and liquids – Solids and liquids

The objectives for this lesson are that students should be able to:

- Identify solids, liquids, and solids that act like liquids

- Group materials as solids or liquids

- Present their findings in a suitable chart

- Make a general rule based on their findings.

SB pp.50–51   *Starter*

- Display a photograph of the solar system. If possible, play some suitable 'space' music to set the mood – the theme music from 'Star Trek' or 'Lost in Space', for example.

- Rig up a pretend first aid box full of 'medicines' in unlabelled containers.

- Present the students with a selection of solids and liquids – include some solids that have small particles and others that are solid blocks; include liquids of varying viscosity. Make sure that some of your solids can't be identified only by sight.

- Tell the students that somewhere, in a galaxy far, far away, the crew of the Starship Venture have a problem...

The challenge

Read the cartoon on page 50 of the *Student Book* together and discuss the problem. Ask the students to come up with as many ways of describing as they can and write them on the board. Encourage them to use as much scientific language as they can; display a word list of useful terms to help them remember.

(Jons Jakob Berzelius was the Swedish chemist who invented the system of representing chemicals with letters.)

What to do

Give groups of students materials to test. How many ways can they find to group their materials?

Take the materials out of their containers. *Can they be poured or piled up? What do they look like under the magnifying glass?*

Heinemann Explore Science

⚠ Although these 'kitchen chemicals' are safe, students should not taste them or put them near their eyes. Ensure they wash their hands thoroughly.

What you need

- A diverse selection of materials to test so that students can group them in different ways. The materials tested on the starship were: cornflour, water, bar of soap, sugar syrup, toffee, custard powder, milk, icing sugar, cooking oil and non-bio washing powder. (This selection is designed to differentiate only between solids and liquids; a more complex experiment to classify six similar looking solids comes later.)

- Water

- Beakers

- Spoons

- Measuring cylinders

- Hand lenses or magnifying glasses.

What to check

Students will have to look and judge very carefully during the investigation. They may have to do several tests to be certain. When looking at the properties of a material or its behaviour, it isn't really necessary to use the same amounts of each, although you may want to encourage the practice to reinforce the principles of fair testing.

Support

Students often become confused when we say we can 'pour' liquids but not solids; after all we do pour solids such as washing powder, sugar and salt. It is less confusing to say that powdered or granular solids can be 'piled up' rather than 'poured'. Show them salt crystals under a microscope to help them realize that fine solids are just like block solids, only smaller.

Liquids will settle with a flat top in a container. Another way of differentiating liquids from fine solids is to use the 'drip test': if you pour a liquid slowly it will form drips as it falls – solids don't.

Extend

All students should be able to distinguish between solid and liquid materials. Some students will be able to rank liquids on the bases of viscosity, although 'runniness' is an acceptable term at this age.

What did you find?

Present

Ask students to present their findings in groups. Students should be encouraged to generalize from their results. As a fallback, they could use the Captain's results given in the *Student Book*. They should find that only some properties are common to all solids and other properties are common to liquids.

Can you do better?

WS 34

Show the students the first part of the Captain's report on WS 34 and read it together. *Do you think this is a good report? Explain your reasons.*

More able students may be able to construct a binary key to classify the ten materials they have. *Do any of the materials look and behave identically?* The students might need to investigate another method of testing.

Now predict

What about jelly, custard, whipped cream, hair gel and ketchup? Well, the answer here is 'it depends'! They are all actually combinations of materials. Tomato sauce is a colloid – a mixture of super-fine solid particles in a liquid in which it does not dissolve. Moisturising lotion and mayonnaise are emulsions where an added ingredient enables oil to spread evenly through water. Lots of materials are mixtures of solids in liquids or gases in liquids – aerosol cream is a liquid mixed with a gas to make what appears to be a solid; leave it for long enough and it will collapse back to liquid form.

Other ideas

Liquid pictures

Mix liquid paint with water until it is really runny. Let the students drop spots of it onto a piece of paper and blow it across the page with a drinks straw. Use different colours and blow the paint in different directions to make tree or seaweed shapes.

How runny?

Have you ever tried to pour a jar of runny honey? It takes forever! Although it's liquid, it is very thick and doesn't pour easily – it has high viscosity. To test viscosity, let the students fill jars with different liquids and drop a marble or piece of Plasticine in each one. The slower the marble falls, the thicker the liquid.

ICT ideas

Plot the viscosity of liquids on a bar chart and use a graphing program to help.

Are the most viscous liquids the most opaque? If you have one, use a light sensor to find out.

At home

WS 35

Ask the students to look at the labels of some common foods like butter, sugar, custard powder, jelly, tomato sauce, mayonnaise, vinegar and cola. Encourage them to look at the list of ingredients. *How many of the foods are made from just one substance? How many are mixtures of several things?*

Ask students to complete WS 35 as homework.

Plenary

Did the Captain do a good job? The end of the story comes in Dissolving solids (pages 58 and 59). Present the students with two new powders (try icing sugar and sodium bicarbonate). *How can we tell them apart? Do they behave differently in water?* Try adding some water. *What if we add a different liquid?* Try vinegar this time and stand back! Sometimes mixing solids and liquids can have explosive results!

Vinegar will have no effect on the sugar but will react with the sodium bicarbonate to produce carbon dioxide gas in a satisfying fizz. You can get the same effect using Epsom salts and water.

73

Unit 4: Separating solids and liquids – Changing materials

The objectives for this lesson are that students should be able to:

- Investigate how materials can be changed by heating and cooling
- Plan and carry out a scientific investigation to test how things change from solids to liquids
- Investigate if some changes can be reversed
- Evaluate whether their predictions were correct.

Starter
SB pp.52–53

- Display a photograph of an ice lolly melting (or the real thing). Show the students a glass of juice with a lolly stick in it. Lament that you'd packed it for your lunch but something must have happened to it. *What could have happened?*
- Show the students a cool box or insulated bag. *Does anyone have one of these at home?* They may have seen them used to carry frozen food home from the supermarket.
- Explain that some materials need to be kept cold to stop them from changing.

The challenge

Read the beginning of page 52 in the *Student Book*. Discuss why some of the party food needed to be kept cold. *Why not all of it? Why do you think Riya's mum suggested putting the chocolate back in the fridge?*

How could we find out which foods melted and which didn't?

What to do

Divide the students into groups and give each group a bowl of fairly hot, but not boiling, water. Put each bowl on a damp tea towel; this will stop it slipping. If you can pre-prepare the food samples you'll save time trying to get the quantities even. Give each group several cake cases with samples of all the foods to test. Ask the students which ones they think will melt the fastest. Let them test each one to see how quickly they melt.

What you need

- Butter, margarine, solid vegetable fat, milk chocolate, dark chocolate, jelly cubes, ice cubes
- Bowls
- Hot tap water or a wheat-filled 'hot water bottle' warmed in the microwave
- Cupcake cases
- Tea towels
- A seconds timer.

What to check

The students need to decide how they are going to measure which food has changed. They could test them all together to see which melts first and last or test them individually using a seconds timer to record the speed, but they need to ensure that the water temperature stays the same. Each way will produce valid results but the students need to choose one method and stick with it. *Where are you going to put the melted foods when you take them out of the water?*

⚠️ The water or 'hot water bottle' you use won't be too hot but remind the students to take care.

Support

Discuss how to make the test fair. Only one variable should be changed, i.e. the food. Everything else should be the same. Make sure the students understand that it is the heat. Decide on what to measure – when the food starts to melt or when it's finished melting completely.

Extend

The students may predict that the hotter the temperature, the faster the fats will melt.

What did you find?
WS 36

Record

The students can use the table provided on WS 36 to record their results.

The students could convert their recorded data into a bar chart. As a fallback, they could use Riya's results given in the *Student Book*. Less able students can present their results visually, representing each food as a competitor in a race, with the one that melts fastest crossing the finishing line first. *Do the foods that melted quickest solidify quickest too?*

Present

Ask the students to present their findings in groups, perhaps using ICT. Encourage them to look at their chart and 'tell its story'.

Can you do better? WS 37 WS 38

Ask students to review how good their evidence was. How would they tackle the investigation differently if they were starting again? For example, a small flag on a cocktail stick in each material will collapse when the material begins to melt.

Use WS 37 to check Riya's results.

Demonstrate what happens when wax melts by lighting a candle and watching the behaviour of the liquid wax. Blow the candle out and see what happens to the wax. Melting wax does not become irreversibly changed but burning wax does. Use WS 38 to record observations.

After taking the foods out of the heat, all but the ice should have returned to a solid state. Different substances melt and freeze at different temperatures and the ice needs to be put in a cold freezer to solidify.

Now predict

Discuss the different possibilities. The students should show an understanding that heating the margarine would cause it to soften and begin to melt which will make it easier to work into the cake mixture.

Other ideas

Chocolate treats

Melt some chocolate. Let the students use it to pour into moulds to make chocolate eggs or mix it with cornflakes to make crispy cakes that will harden when the chocolate cools.

Fabric fun

Batik work is the wax resist technique where melted wax is drawn onto fabric. When the wax sets and the fabric is dyed the waxed parts remain blank. If you have a batik kettle, this is a great art activity to do in small, closely supervised groups.

ICT ideas

Information from this activity can be entered into a graphing program and used to draw a bar chart.

If you have a video recorder with a time-lapse facility, record how the substances melt and invite the students to incorporate it in a PowerPoint display.

At home

Lots of cooking activities involve melting and cooling and the students should be encouraged, with parental or carer support, to become involved in these, e.g. melting chocolate to cover cakes or making jelly.

A no-fuss activity that the students could do themselves at home is to make mini ice lollies using fruit juice or squash. Suggest that they fill ice cube trays with their chosen drink and use a cocktail stick as a stick. If they try different juices they might notice that the liquids containing most sugar take longest to freeze.

Plenary

Remind students of the predictions they made before they started their enquiry. Were they correct? Have the students learned anything that could help with your ice lolly problem? *What could you do to make your ice lolly solid again?*

Unit 4: Separating solids and liquids – Separating materials

The objectives for this lesson are that students should be able to:

- Understand that mixtures can be separated in different ways

- Learn that mixtures of solids and liquids can sometimes be separated

- See how sieving can separate mixtures

- Test which materials make the best filters.

SB pp.54–55 **Starter**

- Display photographs of a colander, sieve and tea strainer (or bring in the real thing).

- Divide the students into groups and ask them to think of a famous person, living or dead.

- Now show them a colander. Give them three minutes to think of as many ways as possible that their person could use this piece of equipment – they can be as silly as they like!

Explain

All mixed up

A mixture is simply two or more materials added together. Mixtures of solids are easiest to spot. Give students a mixture of marbles and salt to separate – of course, this is easy to do because you can just pick out the marbles. Explain that separating a mixture using size is easy when the particles are so big. *What if the mixtures had particles that were closer to each other in size?* Use something like muesli or birdseed mix for the students to try and separate. Give them tweezers and ask them to separate the mixture into different parts; it can certainly be done but they will soon realize that there must be a quicker way!

Sieve it

Sieves come in all shapes and sizes, from garden sieves, used for separating out rocks and stones, to tea strainers. Show the students a selection and emphasize that the important thing to notice is the size of the holes rather than the size of the sieves themselves.

Refer back to the mixture of marbles and salt. *Is it quicker to use a sieve? What would you have to do to separate mixtures of three ingredients?*

Sieves can be used to separate solids of different sizes (such as rice and raisins), to separate the particles in solids with lumps in (such as sifting flour) or to separate insoluble solids from liquids (such as draining vegetables or pasta). Students may have seen all of these types of separation at home.

Paper sieves

Tea strainers are not widely used nowadays but students will probably be familiar with a tea bag. Empty the contents of a tea bag into some hot water in a clear glass. *How can we get the leaves out before we drink it?* Prompt students to think of using a strainer. Then make a cup of tea using a tea bag. Remove the bag and show the students that the solid tea leaves are still in it. Explain that the paper of the tea bag is a mini sieve. Look at an empty tea bag or coffee filter under a microscope or with a lens. *Can you see the tiny holes in it?* Compare this type of paper with writing paper. Point out that it's these holes that let the liquid through but keep the solids behind.

Things to do

Make a mixture

Provide several tubs full of different-sized particles for the students to mix and separate. Good examples are marbles, gravel, dried pasta shapes, sand, salt or sugar, rice, breakfast cereals, dried peas and beans, coins or plastic counters, steel nuts, bolts or screws, and polystyrene balls. Don't provide anything that the students may be tempted to eat!

Record

Ask the students to choose one or two of their most interesting mixtures and to draw the separation sequence they used.

Support

Limit the mixtures to just two very different sizes of particle. Encourage the students to choose the sieve that will retain the largest particles first, e.g. rice and raisins, salt and pasta. Add a third sized particle and help the students to plan the sequence of sieves they need to use to retrieve the largest size first, then the next biggest. Remind them that it is the size of the holes that is important, not the overall size of the sieve.

Extend

Students might like to investigate more complex mixtures or mixtures with particles of similar sizes. Can they extend their knowledge to work out different ways of separation based on criteria other than size? For example, putting it in water can separate a mixture of gravel and puffed rice – the gravel will sink and the puffed rice will float. A mixture of steel paper clips and plastic paper clips can be separated using a magnet. Let them try separating the contents of a dried soup packet.

Filter it out

Try a selection of kitchen towel, paper tissues, paper towels, writing paper, cling film, greaseproof paper and blotting paper.

Record

Set up a display of the different filters you used. Arrange it from the material that provided the clearest water through to the muddiest one.

Support

Let the students look for the holes in the various papers with a hand lens. Point out that the softness of the paper is often a clue too.

Extend

Encourage the students to use other materials such as cotton wool, muslin or even sand.

I wonder...

Take in a fruit juicer from home and show the students how it is designed with troughs and lips to separate the juice from the pips. If Khaled wants to have no pulp in his orange juice, he needs to strain the juice through a filter.

Dig deeper

Ask students to find out why else we use sieves and filters in our everyday lives.

Did you know?

Gunpowder and whipped ice cream are examples of mixtures.

Point out that the hairs in the nose are a natural filter.

Other ideas

Paper making

First, stretch a net curtain across a wooden frame to make a fine sieve for some home-made paper to dry on. Let the students help you mix up a pulp of spare paper (soft paper works best) and water. Spread the gloop over your frame. The water will drop through the net sieve and the paper pulp will stay on the surface. Let it dry. Rolling it when damp will make the paper thinner.

Presentation

Make a collection of different grades of sieve. Label them to show what materials they are used to separate.

At home

WS 39 WS 40

Ask the students to find out where their nearest recycling point is. Discuss how we are encouraged to separate our rubbish into paper, plastic, glass and metal and what happens to these materials after we have done the first stage of sorting.

Ask students to complete WS 39 and WS 40 as homework.

Plenary

Picasso may well have used his sieve as a paintbrush holder or a hat but now the students know what they are really used for! Ask them to write instructions for someone who has never seen one. They must describe what a sieve is used for and how to use it.

Unit 4: Separating solids and liquids – Heating and cooling

The objectives for this lesson are that students should be able to:

- Understand that the same material can exist at different temperatures

- Find out that water can exist in three states – solid, liquid and gas

- Test how water evaporates and what it leaves behind

- Make a presentation using ICT to show how some solids mix and some don't.

SB pp.56–57   *Starter*

- Have several ice cubes ready and challenge the students to lift an ice cube up from the table, using a piece of thread. After several attempts at tying the thread around the ice cube and failing to lift it, they'll probably give up.

- Explain that water is a very strange and unusual substance; what they are about to discover will help them solve the ice cube problem.

Explain

Turning up the heat

Melting a solid turns it into a liquid. Freezing a liquid turns it into a solid. Different materials have different melting and freezing points. Although we tend to associate the word 'freezing' with low temperatures this is not always true. Wax, for example, becomes solid at room temperature. Aluminium melts at 660°C and iron at 1500°C.

Disappearing acts

Melting needs one substance and heat – it is a change of state. Dissolving needs two substances – heat isn't essential but it helps to speed the process up.

When you add a spoonful of sugar to your tea and stir, it spreads out evenly through the water. The sugar (the solute) has dissolved in the water (the solvent) and formed a solution. Soluble solids like salt or sugar mix perfectly in water and form a transparent solution. Demonstrate that particles are still there by letting students taste safe solutions. Solids that do not dissolve perfectly, but hang

in the water without settling to the bottom form suspensions, such as muddy water or flour in water.

Students sometimes can't believe that the solute is still present, particularly as the volume of liquid doesn't increase. You can add a surprisingly large amount of salt to a cup of water before the solution becomes saturated (unable to dissolve any more solid). Demonstrate, by pouring half a cup of salt into half a cup of dried beans, that the sugar or salt in the water has gone into the spaces between the water molecules (the dried beans).

Water, water everywhere

Water is generally found as a liquid. Heating and cooling water will change its state. At temperatures below 0°C it will change into a solid, at 100°C it will boil and change to a gas.

Other liquids which contain little or no water behave differently at these temperatures. White spirit, for example, will not freeze in a domestic freezer and boils at much lower temperatures than water – NOT one to try!

Things to do

Water marks

This activity demonstrates that there are substances dissolved in water that we can't see. The water evaporates – becomes a gas.

Record

Students could draw the pattern of rings left in their dish. If they can look at the particles under a microscope, they could draw the patterns in close-up.

Support

Explain that the water has dried up and left behind things that were dissolved in it. As the minerals are no longer dissolved we can see them.

Extend

Ask the students to find out more about what is added to tap water. *Do you live in an area where fluoride is added to your water supply?*

Kitchen chemistry

Water isn't the only substance in which things dissolve. Oil paint, for example, will dissolve in turpentine but not water, and no amount of water will get rid of a stain from a ballpoint pen! Salt dissolves in water, but not in petrol.

Record

Let the students draw and label their insoluble mixtures.

Support

Colour water and let the students drip oil into it. They should get a satisfying separation.

Add some blue colouring to water and fill a pop bottle half with oil and half with blue water. Replace the top and tip the bottle back and forth on its side – you'll get waves like an ocean.

Extend

Let the students make more layers with golden syrup, oil, water and washing-up liquid. They'll stay separate as long as they're added gently by pouring down the sides of the container.

I wonder...

The sea is a solution of mainly salt and water. Adding salt to water lowers its freezing point. In areas near the poles, the sea does get cold enough to freeze but the ice has very little salt in it.

Dig deeper

Find out more information on melting and freezing. You could also demonstrate that adding salt to water lowers its freezing point.

Did you know?

Water is vitally important to us; even our bodies are 70% water. Some countries take clean water for granted but in other parts of the world many people die from drinking polluted water.

Other ideas

Marbling

The fact that oil and water don't mix means that you can float oil-based marbling inks in a water bath or tray. Swirl the colours around and gently lay paper on the surface of the water. Carefully remove the paper and you'll have beautiful marbled paper.

Presentation

Ask students to use word processing and drawing software to explain why some solids mix and some don't. Display their reports with the results from the activities or the pictures they have painted.

At home

Ask the students to find out how much water their home uses in a day. This should be relatively easy if they have a water meter. Tell them that of all the water used in our homes, 35% is flushed down the toilet! We drink less than 1% of what we use. Invite them to think of ways of saving water.

Plenary

The way to lift an ice cube with a piece of thread is to lay the thread on the surface and to pour a little salt over it. The salt will form a salt solution around the thread and the ice here will melt. After a few minutes in the freezer, it will refreeze and your thread will be frozen into the ice cube, allowing you to pick it up!

During winter in cold countries, salt is put on roads to lower the freezing point of water and stop the roads from icing over.

79

Unit 4: Separating solids and liquids – Dissolving solids

The objectives for this lesson are that students should be able to:

- Investigate which solids dissolve in water and which don't

- Plan how to carry out a fair, reliable investigation

- Find out how to get insoluble solids and dissolved solids back

- Present their findings and evaluate their investigation.

SB pp.58–59   Starter

- Demonstrate dye spreading through water. *What can you see?*

- Present the students with containers of water, salt water and flat lemonade. *They all look the same, but are they?* Ask a volunteer to taste the liquids. *Can you tell the difference between them? What do you think has been added? Where has the sugar or salt gone? Why can't we see it?*

The challenge

Read the cartoon on page 58 of the *Student Book*. Then discuss some ideas with the students. Make sure they understand what 'dissolve' means.

What to do

Decide how to organize the test. Is everyone going to test all of the substances? Encourage the students to work systematically through the samples and to record their results as they find them. Too often, students want to get on with the mixing and neglect the recording, and then they forget which mixture is which. Make sure that they have completed and recorded each test before they move on to another sample.

What you need

- A selection of safe white solids; the ones in the Captain's experiment were flour, large white sugar crystals, uncooked white rice, washing powder, salt, white powder paint

- Measuring cylinders

- Transparent beakers

- A teaspoon

- Funnels

- Filter paper

- A magnifying glass or hand lens

- A seconds timer

- A petri dish or saucer.

Any safe white solids will do for this experiment – you'll be surprised just how many there are. Make sure you have only one that will dissolve completely – granulated sugar or salt are safe bets. Use large sugar crystals to demonstrate that the smaller the size of particle, the quicker it will dissolve. Icing sugar contains a white material that does not dissolve. Its suspension colours the sugar solution.

What to check

Support

Encourage students to measure the water accurately – revise how to use a measuring cylinder. Show the students how to get a level teaspoon of the sample solid by scraping a ruler over the rim of the teaspoon.

Extend

The students may realize that some of the powders have formed a suspension. Let them test for this by holding some text on the far side of the beaker and seeing if they can read it through the mixture.

What did you find?   WS 41

Record

The students could record their data in the table provided on WS 41 or create their own tables. You could use a video time lapse to record how your insoluble solids or suspensions settle during the course of the day.

Present

Ask the students to present their findings in groups.

Can you do better?

WS 42

Ask the students how good their evidence was. How could they tackle the investigation differently if they were starting again?

What else could the students test as part of this investigation? They might consider the temperature of the water, the amount of stirring or no stirring at all, the size of particles or the amount of solid used.

Sample 5 is D51. Read the second part of the Captain's report and complete WS 42. Ask the students to explain their conclusions.

Now predict

Large insoluble solids, like the rice, can be retrieved using a sieve or strainer. Filter paper can separate solids that have partly dissolved or formed suspensions. The liquid will pass through the paper leaving the solid residue in the filter. This works for a suspension like flour. Only boiling or evaporating can separate the dissolved salt. Demonstrate this by making up a very strong salt solution and pouring it into a large, shallow dish. Leave it on a windowsill or radiator to speed up the evaporation process. Let the students examine the salt crystals that form using a microscope or lens. The powder paint can be retrieved in the same way but it will be changed slightly.

Separating salt and sand can be done in a couple of stages. Add water to the mixture to dissolve the salt, put this mix through a filter to remove the sand and then evaporate the water in the separated salt solution to leave salt behind.

Other ideas

Create a crystal

Make a crystal chain by tying a piece of thread to a pencil and suspending it in a jar containing a saturated solution. Copper sulphate or alum both make good crystals. Copper sulphate is not recommended for students' use so use it for

demonstration, but alum, a mildly astringent disinfectant, is not poisonous. Rock salt can give good results too and is safe for students to use. The slower the evaporation rate and the cleaner the container and tools used, the larger your crystals will be.

Separating colours

Water-soluble inks in felt-tipped pens can be separated into their component colours by chromatography. Mark a blob of colour near the bottom of a piece of filter paper or kitchen paper and suspend the end in water. As the water soaks up the paper, the different colours of ink will separate out. Black is the best colour to try. If the ink doesn't separate, then it must be made from only one pigment. If the ink doesn't spread out, then it may be spirit-based.

ICT ideas

Students can investigate the effects of temperature on dissolving. Let them try dissolving sugar in water of different temperatures. They should keep adding sugar until no more will dissolve and record the temperatures of the water samples. *Does the warmest water dissolve the most solid?* If you have one, let students use a temperature sensor to record the temperatures and plot their results on a spreadsheet.

At home

WS 43

Ask the students to complete WS 43, which revises learning, as homework.

Plenary

Ask the students to imagine that they are the owner of a coffee bar. They're trying to decide which sugar to put on the tables. They have several types to choose from and want the sugar that dissolves the fastest. *What variables do you need to think about? How would you test the sugars?*

Unit 4: Separating solids and liquids – Unit 4 Review

The objectives for this lesson are that students should be able to:

- Check what they have learned about states of matter in this Unit

- Find out how they are working towards, within and beyond the Grade 4 level.

SB p.60   *Expectations*

Students working towards Grade 4 level will:

- Name some solids and liquids

- Describe that when ice melts it turns to a liquid

- Recognize that common solids become liquid when heated and vice versa

- Recognize that salt or sugar dissolves in water but sand won't

- Separate an undissolved solid from a liquid by filtering.

In addition, students working within Grade 4 level will:

- Describe the differences between solids and liquids

- Describe melting and dissolving and give everyday examples of each

- Name some materials that will and some that will not dissolve in water

- Explain why undissolved solids can be separated from a solution by filtering and show how to do this

- Recognize that although it is not possible to see a dissolved solid it remains in the solution

- Recognize that filtering cannot separate dissolved solids/solutions

- Make careful relevant observations and comparisons

- Decide what was discovered.

Further to this, students working beyond Grade 4 level will also:

- State that some materials, e.g. metals, have to be heated to a very high temperature before they melt

- Explain that when solids dissolve they break up so small they pass through the holes in the filter paper

- Begin to evaluate the evidence.

Check-up

Hassan and Jamal need to separate rice, salt and flour. First, they can separate the rice, which has the largest particles, from the dry solids by using a sieve. This is separation based on size. Next, they need to mix the flour and salt with water. The salt will dissolve in the water making a salt solution. Some of the flour will settle and some will float in suspension. The boys now need to filter this mixture. The solid flour will be trapped in the filter but the salt solution will pass through. The water should then be evaporated off the salt solution to leave salt crystals behind.

Assessment   WS 44

Use the Unit 4 assessment on WS 44 to check the students' understanding of the content of the Unit. The answers are given opposite.

Name: _____   Date: _____

WS 44   Unit 4 assessment

1 Circle the solid materials.

paper	water	air	sand	sugar cube
milk	ice	plastic ruler	rain	tree

2 Mansoor dropped some materials onto a hot frying pan. He wrote down what he saw in this table.

Name the materials that show solids changing to liquids.

Material	What I saw
chocolate drop	spreads out
plain biscuit	did not move, no change
butter	spreads out, starts to bubble
cooking oil	spreads out

3 What do we call the process when a solid changes to a liquid?

4 What would Mansoor need to do to turn the liquids solid again?

5 What equipment would you use to separate a mixture of flour and raisins?

6 Explain what happens when a substance dissolves in water.

7 Circle the equipment you would use to separate a mixture of sand and water.

sieve	filter paper	colander

44   Heinemann Explore Science Grade 4

Answers

1   Paper, sand, sugar cube, ice, plastic ruler, tree

2   Butter and chocolate

3   Melting

4   Freeze/cool them

5   A sieve

6   Accept an explanation that mentions that the substance seems to disappear and that it is now spread evenly through the liquid in a transparent solution.

7   Filter paper

The answer!

Students should now be aware that just because they cannot see particles in a solution doesn't mean that there is nothing there. Toxic waste is pretty rare these days although a favourite with students when asked to name pollutants. More common pollutants are fertilizers, detergents and sewage which reduce the oxygen levels in water and make it difficult for fish and other creatures to survive.

And finally...

Ask students to talk through the stages in making a cup of sweet milky tea. Ask them to explain what is happening, scientifically, at each stage from boiling the water to lifting the cup.

New International Edition

Unit 5: Gases around us

The objectives for this Unit are that students should be able to:

- Understand that gases are materials and have weight

- Make and repeat scientific observations

- Find out how gas particles move and can change state

- Explain the differences between gases, solids and liquids.

SB p.61 **Science background**

At this level students are required to know about the three states of matter in more detail. Role-play activities can be very successful in putting across the differences. Explain how the particles are arranged and how they move in each state; then ask the students to behave like particles.

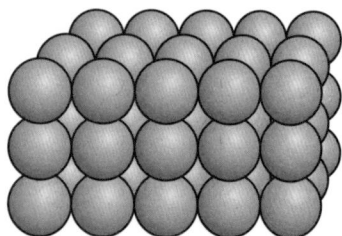

Solid particles are closely packed together in a regular pattern. The particles vibrate about fixed points only.

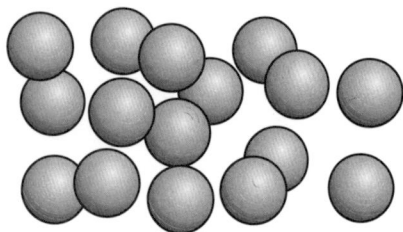

Particles in a liquid are still touching, but are not regularly arranged. They also have more energy so are moving around each other all the time, which is why they can flow.

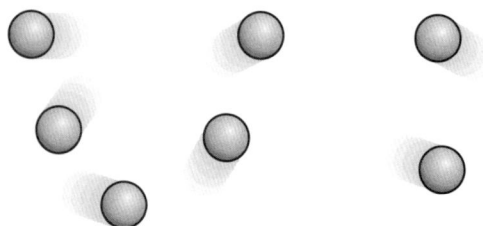

Gas particles move very fast, in a rapid random motion. They change direction from their straight line path when they collide with another particle or the sides of whatever container they are in – a balloon skin or a classroom wall. There is space between each particle.

As you give solid particles energy – usually by heating – they will move faster and change from solid to liquid, then to gas. You can sense this transfer of energy if you pour a liquid on your hand – it feels cold as it gains energy and may evaporate as gas.

These arrangements of particles explain their properties. A solid keeps its shape, but a liquid flows, as does a gas. Solids can't be squashed as there is little space between the particles, but liquids can be compressed a little and gases much more.

Sounds travel fastest through solids as the sound energy can be passed quickly from one particle to the next as they are close together. Diffusion (the movement of one set of particles through another) happens fastest in a gas. Here there is more space between particles for the new substance to move through, as it will be pushed along faster by the very fast moving gas. Gas particles move as fast as a bullet leaving a rifle!

Language	
Air	A mixture of gases.
Carbon dioxide	A waste product of respiration and burning. Used by plants for photosynthesis.
Chlorine	Gas used to keep swimming pool water clean.
Condensation	The process when a gas turns back to a liquid. Often seen on windows in winter, as the water vapour in air in the house condenses on the cold window.
Evaporation	When a liquid becomes a vapour or gas.
Gas	A state of matter made of very fast moving and spread out particles.
Helium	Inert (non-flammable) gas which is less dense than air. Used in gas balloons.

Hydrogen	Flammable gas, once used for balloons and airships.
Natural gas	Used for heating, cooking and Bunsen burners.
Oxygen	Gas needed by almost all life for respiration.
Particles	Very small pieces of material.

The Words to learn list on page 61 of the *Student Book* can be used to make a classroom display.

Resources

- *Solids, Liquids and Gases* Reader
- Sponge
- Measuring cylinders or other vessels
- Marbles or other small spherical objects that can be packed together
- A range of soils
- Fizzy lemonade in a transparent plastic bottle
- Perfume
- Air freshener
- Several plastic syringes, sealed at the small end, containing (separately) water, air and sand
- Balloons
- Wire coat-hangers
- Blu-tack
- Sticky tape
- A digital balance
- A range of solids and liquids.

Bright ideas

- Hand lenses or microscopes are good for observing the structure of soils.
- A moisture sensor, either computer-linked or hand-held, is useful for checking the water content of soils.

Knowledge check

- The students will already have met the term 'volume' and will have measured liquids. But

volume relates to all three states of matter, not just liquids, which is probably the only context they have encountered so far.

- This Unit consolidates differences between solids and liquids and introduces gases. These are harder to recognize as they are often odourless and colourless as well as transparent.

Skills check

Students need to:

- make observations and repeat those observations
- relate their observations to their conclusions and their scientific understanding.

Some students will:

- explain why observations and measurements need to be repeated
- recognize and make clear distinctions between solids, liquids and gases.

Links to other subjects

Literacy:	Reading and following simple instructions, e.g. carrying out the investigations.
Numeracy:	Reading scales, e.g. measuring cylinders. Organizing and interpreting simple data in bar graphs or line graphs.
ICT:	Using a multi-media package to combine text and graphics to make a presentation.
Personal Social Health Education (PSHE):	Taking care of yourself – recognizing the dangers of some gases.

Let's find out...

The Unit opens with this question:

If you put a house brick in water, bubbles come out of it. What are these bubbles? Where have they come from?

85

Unit 5: Gases around us – Solids, liquids and gases

The objectives for this lesson are that students should be able to:

- Revise the differences between solids and liquids

- Understand that gas has mass and can be weighed

- Explain their experiment on weighing air and the results they found

- Take part in a presentation using drama.

SB pp.62–63   *Starter*

- Remind students of a range of solids and liquids and ask them to sort them. Include sand and flour as well as wax, cork, metals, water, tomato ketchup, etc. *How did you group them?* If they didn't do it by state of matter, then ask them to sort them a different way.

- Write the words 'solid' and 'liquid' on the board, dividing the board in two. Ask the students what words or ideas or examples they can think of for each. Look for a description of their properties and examples of each.

- Blow up a balloon. Ask the students what is filling the balloon. *Why can you go on blowing over and over again? Where does all this air go? Why couldn't you keep pouring jugs of water into it?* Draw out the understanding that air (a gas) can be compressed (squashed or squeezed) inside the balloon. *It must really exist – otherwise why would the balloon go on getting bigger?*

Explain

Set in its ways

The students have already investigated powders in Grade 4 so should be able to explain why, although it pours like a liquid, a powder is a solid. If not, ask them to look at some sand under a microscope or hand lens. Point out that each grain is solid. Pour some sand onto the desk to show that it won't run over the desk like a liquid. If the students still need clarification, use sugar lumps. They should all agree that the sugar lump is a solid. If you put a lot of them into a cup, you can 'pour' them out.

Are they solid or liquid? Explain that the grains of sand are like small versions of the lumps of sugar and that flour has even smaller grains.

Wind

If you have a hand fan, turn it on. Ask the students what is happening and what they feel. *Where does the wind come from? Does it just appear or is it always there?* The students will have felt air resistance when they were doing work on friction. If necessary, repeat the activity of running with a large card, or even drop some gyrocopters. Even when the wind isn't blowing, there is still air about. Ask the students what they breathe in. *Where is it? If there wasn't any air would we be alive?*

Things to do

Gas has mass

This is a very simple and effective activity to carry out. However, you should be aware that the inflated balloon has more mass because it has more air in it than the apparently empty one. The 'empty' one does have air in it, but the pressure is equal inside and outside, so the rubber doesn't stretch. When you blow into the balloon you are forcing more and more air particles in. They collide with the walls of the balloon, creating air pressure. As there are more particles packed in the inflated balloon, it weighs more.

Record

The students could draw a diagram of the apparatus used and explain why the inflated balloon pulls the coat-hanger down on that side.

Support

Achieving balance is tricky. Part of the activity is for the students to put the air into the balloon. Some students might query the fairness of the sticky tape. Measure 5 cm per balloon to avoid causing any discrepancies.

Extend

All students should see that the inflated balloon pulls the coat-hanger down on that side, showing the compressed air has mass.

Some students could try to balance two balloons full of air or investigate whether the shape of the balloon makes any difference, by using long balloons and round ones.

I wonder...

If air wasn't transparent, we wouldn't be able to see through it clearly. If it was coloured, everything would look a different colour – like always wearing sunglasses. If it smelled, we'd have to get used to it!

Dig deeper

Capillary action is related to surface tension. Surface tension is the property of particles of liquid attracting each other. It is the principle that allows insects to 'skate' over the surface of ponds – their feet don't break the layer of particles on the surface of the water, which is almost like a 'skin'. If you put a liquid in contact with a very thin tube, called a capillary, the particles of liquid will pull themselves up the tube. The sides of the capillary attract the surface particles of the liquid, which attracts all the other particles in the liquid, so they are all pulled up the tube. This is how plants draw up water and how paper towels absorb water.

Show surface tension by carefully placing some matchsticks in water in a circle with the heads pointing the same way. Put a drop of liquid soap in the centre of the circle and the matches will float away from the centre as the soap breaks the surface tension. The same principle can be used to make a boat – a foil boat with a piece of soap at the back will be propelled forward as the soap breaks the surface tension, causing the particles to repel rather than attract each other.

Did you know?

Helium is the second lightest and second most abundant substance in the universe – after hydrogen. Its light weight makes it ideal for inflating balloons.

Other ideas

Nothing there?

The students could draw pictures of all the places they see the effects of air or wind or where they see it being used, e.g. blowing windmills, kites, seeds and leaves, etc.

Presentation

Let the students put on a play on what life would be like if there wasn't any air, assuming that we could live without oxygen!

Alternatively, they could put a presentation together using PowerPoint.

At home

Ask the students to look at all the places in their home where air is used to do something, e.g. heating, cooking, cooling, etc.

Plenary

Show the students a syringe (without the needle). Hold your finger over the end and prove that there must be something there, as you can't press the plunger in. By removing your finger and depressing the plunger under water, the students can see bubbles, which proves there was something in the syringe. Can they describe what has happened? Can they think of other examples to prove that the air is present and that it weighs something?

Unit 5: Gases around us – Air around us

The objectives for this lesson are that students should be able to:

- Understand that the spaces in solids are filled with a gas, often air

- Learn that gas is often mixed with solids or liquids

- Find out that gas is less dense than liquid as it contains fewer particles

- Make a list of objects that are a mixture of solids and gases.

SB pp.64–65

Starter

- Demonstrate a solid that dissolves in water and one that doesn't. *What could each of the solids be?* Demonstrate a mixture of two liquids with orange cordial and water. *Can you mix two solids?* This is harder, but peas and sand are a mixture, for example. Then explain that gases can form a mixture. Ask the students if they know of any mixtures of gases. Air is a mixture of gases – nitrogen, oxygen, carbon dioxide and small quantities of some rarer, inert gases.

Explain

What's the matter?

This introduces matter as particles. These only need to be likened to very tiny pieces of material. Although the students don't need to know the particle arrangements, they usually grasp the concept well and enjoy the role-play described in the introduction.

Honeycomb chocolate

A science activity based on food is always enjoyable! It relates to everyday life and students find it easier to understand. Break a honeycomb chocolate bar into chunks, to see the holes in it. Ask the students what is in them. They might reply nothing or they might have realized that just because they can't see anything, it doesn't mean there's nothing there.

The honeycomb chocolate bar illustrates a gas trapped in a solid, but you can also have gas trapped in a liquid. Squirty cream or aerosol

shaving foam are good examples. Ask the students to compare fresh cream with the aerosol version. The aerosol version goes 'flat' as the gas bubbles burst and the gas escapes into the air.

Full of fizz

Lemonade is another example of a gas in a liquid. Carbon dioxide gas has been dissolved in the lemonade under pressure. When the cap is released, the gas can escape. The bubbles rise upwards, as they are less dense than the liquid, i.e. there are fewer particles in a gas bubble than in a droplet of liquid of the same volume.

Things to do

Investigate sand and water

Sand and water mixed together take up a smaller volume than sand and water separately, as the water displaces the air. Repeat the exercise to prove what took place or let the students make a prediction, then test to see if they are correct. This shows them the validity of taking more than one set of results to prove that their observations are probably right.

Record

The students could draw a diagram of the sand and water to explain what is happening. They could also take pictures of the investigation with a digital camera. These could then be annotated on the computer and used to produce a report.

Support

Students may find it hard to explain what happens when the water goes on top of the sand. Clear this up with a quick demonstration. Put a couple of layers of marbles into a jar. Add an equal volume of sand. The students probably expect the sand to double the final volume, e.g. 50 ml marbles, plus 50 ml sand = 100 ml marbles and sand. The sand fits in air spaces between the marbles. Explain that the same thing happens with the sand and water, but the particles are smaller.

Extend

All students should understand that the air spaces are filled by the water in the sand.

Most should recognize that if they repeat their investigations and get the same answer, then it is more likely to be correct.

88

Some students could work out the volume of the air in the sand and predict the total volume of water and sand for other initial volumes.

Dig deeper

The air is about one fifth oxygen. All living things need oxygen to respire. Without it life on Earth would die. The air also provides a 'blanket'. It provides a glasshouse effect that is necessary to keep the Earth warm enough for life. Without the atmosphere, the Earth would be too hot during the day. It would lose the accumulated heat during the night. The planet Mercury has no atmosphere and so is very hot in the day and freezing at night.

I wonder...

Kitchen paper and other absorbent materials have small holes in them, or pockets of air, sealed between thin pieces of material. The more absorbent the material, the more air spaces it has to trap liquid.

Did you know?

There are a few particles of gas in space but they are so far apart that they cannot transmit sounds.

Other ideas

High rise

Prove that the volume of a gas has less mass than the same volume of liquid by adapting the coat-hanger activity from the last lesson. This will show why bubbles in lemonade rise. Fill one balloon with water and one with air. The balloon containing water will pull the hanger down on that side, no matter how much air you put into the balloon.

How much air?

Let the students investigate whether bigger holes in a sponge mean that it produces more bubbles or just bigger ones. In a design and technology lesson, they could design a device to capture the gas and measure its volume instead of the number of bubbles. As gas rises due to its lack of density compared to a liquid, the best way to collect the gas is by forcing it into an upturned vessel that is full of water. The gas will displace the water so the volume of gas can be measured.

Half full?

Let the students discuss whether a cup is 'half full or half empty'. Do they mean different things?

Presentation

If the students took digital pictures of their investigations, let them incorporate them into a PowerPoint presentation of their findings. During the presentation, they should say how important it is to repeat the investigation to check their observations.

At home

WS 45

Ask the students to make a list of all the objects in their home that are a mixture of solids and gases. They should be looking for foams and foods like leavened bread.

Ask students to complete WS 45 as homework.

Plenary

Show the students some solids. Ask them to make predictions, based on their previous results, as to whether the objects contain any air.

Unit 5: Gases around us – Air in the soil

The objectives for this lesson are that students should be able to:

- Discover what worms and other soil creatures need to live

- Plan and carry out a scientific investigation on which soil has the most air

- Make predictions on which soil has the most air spaces

- Explain why repeating their investigation might be valuable.

SB pp.66–67

Starter

- Look at the photo of the earthworm in soil on page 67 of the *Student Book*. Discuss what worms need to live. *Why do worms need air spaces in soil?*

- Place a large number of plastic counters or marbles on an overhead projector. Ask the students to count them. Point out of the window to divert their attention and either add or remove some counters. Then ask the students to count again. This activity will help to show why it is important to check your results and not just take things for granted.

The challenge

Read the opening of page 66 in the *Student Book*. Discuss with the students why the earthworm needs the air, i.e. it needs the oxygen in it to breathe. It will not survive in soil without air spaces.

Talk about the different types of soils they met in Grade 3. *Which type contains the most air spaces? How can you tell?*

What to do

The experimental procedure is similar to that used in the last lesson with the sand and water. The students should make the connection that if they are looking at air spaces, the way to 'measure' them is by seeing how much water can fill those spaces. All three ideas are valid, but only the second two give measurable results.

What you need

- Measuring cylinders

- At least three different types of soil – use the ones from the rocks and soils investigations

- Water.

⚠️ The soil must be from an area free from litter or animal waste or faeces. The students must wash their hands after handling the soil.

What to check

To make this investigation fair, the students will need to agree on the volume of soil and water they are going to use.

Support

Some students may need help in explaining their results. The investigation itself is quite straightforward. The more air in the soil, the more spaces there are for the water to get into, so the less total volume there is. Demonstrate this with different sized marbles and water, as with the marbles and sand in the last lesson. Large marbles leave large air spaces, so the total volume is less.

Extend

All students should be able to measure their volumes accurately.

Most students should be able to recognize that the more air spaces, the lower the final volume.

Some students could repeat their investigation and work out the average of their results. They could then explain why they have repeated it and taken an average.

Some students could repeat their investigation using different volumes of soil and water to see if the effect is the same.

What did you find?

WS 46

The students could use WS 46 to record the total volume of water needed to fill each container. They can also produce a graph. This data should produce a bar chart of results.

Record

As a fallback, they could use the group's data, given in the *Student Book*. More able students, who have repeated the investigation and also taken an average of their results, could present their data as a bar graph.

Present

Let each group of students present their findings. They should include their table of results and charts or graphs. The bar chart should show which total volume was the smallest. The students will need to explain this in terms of the water pushing the air out of the spaces and filling it. The more air spaces, the more water can get in, so less water sits on top of the soil.

Can you do better?

WS
47

Use WS 47 to decide on the best soil to use for a wormery. Idealised figures are given.

Now predict

If soil contains lots of air spaces, it is free draining. Sand is free-draining; clay is not. If the soil gets waterlogged, then it will be very compact. This relates to Grade 3 work on rocks and soils.

Other ideas

How much water?

An alternative way to gain results would be to keep adding water until the soil is just covered, then calculate the volume that has been used. This involves filling the measuring cylinder accurately, then reading off how much has been poured out. The students could repeat the investigation, using the information gained in the first trial, of adding that volume of water to the soil, to check if it is correct.

ICT ideas

Let the students look at the different soil samples under a digital microscope to observe the air space. *Are they easy to see?* The students could then make predictions based on these observations about how much air a particular soil, or any solid, has in it.

The students could measure the moisture content of various soils with a moisture sensor linked to the computer. Can they use this information to predict which soil to use in the wormery?

At home

Ask the students to look at the types of packaging that is used to keep things cold. For example, supermarkets use expanded polystyrene which contains gas bubbles for food trays.

Plenary

Ask the students why it is important to check their results. Encourage them to think of a situation in real life where they check things to make sure, e.g. counting their money twice.

New International Edition

Unit 5: Gases around us – Different gases

The objectives for this lesson are that students should be able to:

- Understand that there are lots of different gases

- Consider why different gases are used and what their properties are

- Find that some gases are harmful and some are helpful

- Research the constituents of air and display their findings.

SB pp.68–69   Starter

- Display a photo of helium filled balloons (or bring in the real thing) and any other examples of gases, e.g. lemonade, a gas cylinder from a camping stove.

- Discuss with the students all the ways in which the word 'gas' is used in our society. *What is 'gas'?* It is a state of matter. But we use the word 'gas' to mean other things. 'Gas' to the Americans is what others call petrol. They have shortened the word 'gasoline'. If you cook on 'gas' you use butane or propane or natural gas, all of which are real gases.

Explain

Gas-tastic!

These gases are transparent, colourless and odourless. But pictures of the gases being used will help prove that they exist and are useful to us.

Discuss with the students why these gases are used. This means looking at their properties, like density and flammability.

Gas attack

The *Student Book* given explains that some gases can be harmful if not used correctly. Another common harmful gas is sulphur dioxide; this is produced by burning petrol. It has a choking smell and in larger quantities makes your eyes water. It is also corrosive and a component of acid rain.

Things to do   WS 48   WS 49

Gas disaster!

Refer students to WS 48 containing Professor Vapour's remaining notes. Also use WS 49. The information on page 68 of the *Student Book* helps with this activity.

Record

The information from the Professor can either be recorded as a table of data or on cards that give information about each of the gases. A template for the cards is on WS 49.

Students could produce a leaflet about one particular gas. The leaflets are then built into a display.

Support

Students could record their information on gases on the card templates using the necessary information collected on WS 48.

Extend

All students should know that there are many different gases and some of them are useful to us.

Some students could 'adopt' and research a particular gas further using text books or the Internet.

I wonder...

We breathe air – a mixture of gases – and oxygen is only one-fifth of it. Rarely, some people may be given pure oxygen in medical treatment. It is used for activities at high altitudes or in deep sea diving. Breathing concentrated oxygen is beneficial in illnesses of the lungs and cardiovascular system. There is no evidence to prove that breathing pure oxygen by healthy people at sea level does any good to them. In fact it could weaken breathing and the movement of cilia, the tiny hairs that protect our nose and lungs.

Dig deeper

Hydrogen is the lightest gas known on Earth. It is an element and can be made or found naturally. It is highly flammable. The airship *Hindenberg* was filled with hydrogen, which lifted it into the sky.

However, in a terrible disaster the airship caught fire and burnt out. Helium is now used in gas balloons, because it is not inflammable. It is nearly as light as hydrogen. Neon, argon and krypton are related to helium. They are inert gases. Argon is the gas in many light bulbs.

Compressed gas becomes liquid. So gases are moved in containers that hold liquid gas. Opening the valve reduces the pressure, the liquid evaporates and gas is released.

Did you know?

Find out more on some gases and their uses and properties.

Other ideas

Natural mixture

Encourage the students to research the constituents of air and draw a graph of the relative proportions. A pie chart would be hard, but not impossible, for more able students. The values are:

- 78% nitrogen, which is fairly unreactive

- 21% oxygen, which is essential to life

- a small amount of argon, which is very unreactive (and is used in light bulbs)

- a small amount of carbon dioxide, as used in fire extinguishers and fizzy drinks.

Environmentally friendly

Let the students research the gases that harm the Earth's atmosphere, e.g. sulphur dioxide, excess carbon dioxide and chlorofluorocarbons (CFCs). They could look at how to reduce their production or counteract what has been done already.

Presentation

With the students' help, use the information on gases to produce a wall display of different gases and their properties. Depending on how much information the students have collected, this could be in the form of information cards, a poster or leaflets.

The students could perform a play on what life would be like without certain gases, e.g. without chlorine swimming pools couldn't be kept clean enough for us to swim in.

At home

Ask the students to find information about at least one gas that causes pollution or environmental damage. *How is it made?*

Plenary

Show some objects that use gas, or pictures of them, and ask the students what property that they think the gas has, e.g. flammable, not flammable, light, smell, etc.

93

Unit 5: Gases around us – Moving gases

The objectives for this lesson are that students should be able to:

- Understand that all liquids evaporate to form gases

- Test how evaporation works on puddles

- Investigate perfume to see how it evaporates and what they can smell

- Draw a representation of how liquid evaporates and turns into gas.

SB pp.70–71

Starter

- Show a photo of a perfume bottle or bring in the real thing. *How does the smell get from the bottle to your nose?*

- Remind students of how they know what is for lunch, even when they are miles from the kitchen. *How does the smell of food make you feel towards lunchtime?*

- Put a variety of objects in opaque bags and ask the students what they think is in each, or ask them to close their eyes and guess, just using their sense of smell. Include things like oranges, soap, pot pourri and cooked vegetables. *How do you know what is in the bag? How can the smell reach your nose?*

Explain

Mmmmm!

To show that the smell is made of particles and moves through the air, spray some air freshener at one end of the room. *Put your hand up when you can smell it!* At first only students close to you will react. Eventually, all the students will smell it, proving that the smell does move through the air.

Now you see it...

Use a few drops of aftershave on saucers to show this happening. The solvent will evaporate much faster than water, so the effect is easy to see. It is said to be more volatile.

... now you don't

Evaporation will happen even faster if you place a droplet of aftershave on your hand. The warmth of your hand provides the liquid particles with enough energy to escape the liquid, so entering the air and forming a vapour. You feel the resulting coldness.

Things to do

Rain and shine

Pour a bucket of water onto the playground in an area where puddles can form. Alternatively, set up a shallow tray of water on a window sill or near an air-conditioning vent. If possible, take pictures with a digital camera each time that the puddle is marked.

Record

The students can draw a diagram of the puddle with the chalk marks on, showing how the puddle gets smaller with time. If they mark the time on each chalk line, they can predict where a line would be drawn for a time between the times marked or for future evaporation.

Support

As the puddles take a long time to evaporate, some students may well lose interest. As an alternative, set a range of different things to dry, e.g. a paper towel, a tea towel or water in a saucer. The students could feel them to see what happens. This shows how water evaporates from wet surfaces.

Extend

All students will observe that the liquid water 'disappears'.

Most students should conclude that the water has evaporated and is now in the air.

Some students could work out the amount of water that has evaporated, in simple terms, by measuring the greatest diameter of the puddle each time they draw the chalk line. More able students could attempt to estimate the volume.

I wonder...

Cooking gas is flammable. It is also poisonous when not lit. An artificial smell may be added to detect the gas if it leaks. People could either die from poisoning, or from the gas building up and exploding.

Dig deeper

Your nose has receptors in it that detect particles, then send signals to your brain. The particles are like keys that fit the 'locks' of the detectors. Your brain determines what the smell is and tells your body how to react to it. Food smells can make you salivate; a bad smell will have you holding your breath. Some of our behaviour reactions to smells are learned, some instinctive. Many insects have sensors on antennae to pick up the chemical information that an odour can give them.

Did you know?

Taste and smell are closely linked. Loss of the sense of smell affects taste.

Other ideas

What's that smell?

Place a saucer of (cheap) perfume at the front of the class, so the students can all see the liquid. *What can you smell? How is the smell reaching you? What will happen to it if it is left?* Ask the students to look at the perfume carefully. *Can you see the perfume evaporating? If you look closely, can you see a shimmering?* Explain that this is the vapour leaving the liquid and moving into the air. Encourage the students to draw a cartoon strip to show how the perfume particles leave the perfume and travel through the air to their nose so they can be smelled. They have already found that it takes longer for the smell to reach the back of the room.

Presentation

If you took digital pictures of the puddle, let the students use them as part of a PowerPoint presentation to show what happens to a liquid in dry and warm conditions. If you can leave a video camera filming the puddle during an afternoon, you could speed up the film to show it evaporating. Encourage the students to incorporate a description of what is happening.

At home

Suggest to the students that when they next do some washing-up at home, they leave half the plates to dry on their own and dry the other half with a tea towel. *What happens to the water on the plates? What happens to the water in the tea towel? Do they all get dry? Why do plates washed in hot water dry faster than plates washed in cold water?*

Plenary

Show a range of safe liquids and ask the students if they smell. Discuss why it is important that we can smell them. We can often tell what something is from its smell alone. It is important to be able to smell something that will be harmful to us so that we can avoid it.

Unit 5: Gases around us – States of matter

The objectives for this lesson are that students should be able to:

- Describe the differences between solids, liquids and gases

- Explain changes of state

- Produce an identity card for each state of matter, explaining its properties

- Consider how heat affects and changes matter.

SB pp.72–73

Starter

- Show a range of materials, including Plasticine, treacle or sugar syrup, and toothpaste. Discuss whether they are solids, liquids or gases.

Explain

What a state!

Place an ice cube on your desk and ask the students to point out the three states of matter. They will probably point to the water and the ice. *Where is the water vapour?* Encourage the students to use solid, liquid and gas even for water, although water has special names for its solid and gaseous states (i.e. ice and steam). Note that visible steam is not really water gas. It is water vapour – particles of liquid water in the air. Water is a gas only when it is hotter than its boiling point – hotter than 100°C. Water gas (true steam) is invisible.

Squidgy

The only solids that will be squidgy are those that have a gas – usually air – in them. The air is being compressed, or even forced out, by the solid trying to occupy the space it took up. Common solids that can be compressed are sponges and some balls.

Liquids are difficult to compress as the particles are almost as closely packed as in a solid, but have the freedom to move around each other, hence they flow but don't take up much more volume than the related solid.

Gases are highly compressible as the particles are so spread out that they can be forced closer together.

Things to do

What's the difference?

Students will need a variety of shaped containers and a measuring cylinder or jug, so that they can measure the volume of liquid after pouring it – proof that the volume remains unchanged.

Set up sealed syringes with a solid, like sand: one containing water and one with a gas.

> ⚠ It is very important that the syringes are counted back. You can seal the syringes with little rubber caps or sticky tape, but the force the students put onto them can cause them to 'blow'. If you use syringes provided by a high school, ask the technician to seal them over a Bunsen burner, so they are not useable for anything but this activity.

Use some liquids that are volatile, e.g. paint, perfume, tincture of iodine, in their containers so the students can observe the movement of the vapour once the top has been removed, proving that gases flow.

Record

The students could draw a diagram of the apparatus they used to prove the property, e.g. different shaped vessels with coloured water in them, all reading the same volume.

Support

Ask the students not to pull the plungers out of the syringes, as they are fiddly to make up and you don't want sand or water everywhere. *Which state can you squash the most? Does the volume of a liquid change when you pour it? Does a solid need a container? What happens to the vapour when you open a tin of paint?*

Try using coloured water for the liquid; it makes it easier to see what is happening.

Extend

Some students can test the difference between different liquids or different solids, e.g. water and milk and wood and plastic. *Are there any differences? Why?*

I wonder...

The students may notice that tiny water droplets appear in the end of the syringe. This is because the gas particles have been squashed so much that they liquefy.

Dig deeper

An energy change accompanies a change of state. If you want the substance to change from a solid to a liquid or a liquid to a gas, you have to add heat energy. This causes the particles to move faster and spread out more. When a material changes from gas to liquid or from liquid to solid, heat energy is lost.

Did you know?

These facts show that there are some substances that are a little different from the others in their state group.

Other ideas

Identity card

The students could produce an identity card for each state of matter, writing down the main facts.

Identity parade

Use the identity card idea to produce a game. On one series of cards, let the students draw diagrams of the apparatus or idea used to prove the property. On another set, let them write the property that it proves. For instance, on one card, a diagram of a syringe; on another card, the words 'gases can be squashed'. The students can then use the cards in a memory type game, matching the two sets of cards together.

How useful!

If you have a space hopper show how useful it is that gases can be squashed. If there wasn't any air in the space hopper, you couldn't bounce on it.

Presentation

Ask students to work in groups of three, each one representing a 'state of matter' to explain the differences between them.

At home

WS 50

Ask the students to look for places where the use of state is appropriate to its use, e.g. a car – the petrol is a liquid that will fill the tank, the tyres are filled with air to absorb shocks and the car body is made of a solid to keep its shape.

Ask the students to complete WS 50 as homework.

Plenary

Pour some water on your desk. Ask the students which way it flows. Take the top off a perfume bottle or air freshener and ask the students which way the gas will flow. Invite the students to spread out around the room, under and over desks and at the back of the room. The water will only flow across the desk, but the perfume vapour can be smelled above and below the desks, as well as throughout the room.

Unit 5: Gases around us – Unit 5 Review

The objectives for this lesson are that students should be able to:

- Check what they have learned about gases around us in this Unit

- Find out how they are working towards, within and beyond the Grade 4 level.

Expectations

Students working towards Grade 4 level will:

- State that air is a gas

- Recognize that gases flow from place to place and measure volumes of liquid.

In addition, students working within Grade 4 level will:

- Recognize that air is a material and that it is one of a range of gases which have important uses

- Recognize that liquids evaporate to form gases and that gases change shape and flow from place to place

- Measure volumes of liquids accurately, recognize when observations and measurements need to be repeated

- Provide explanations for what they observe in terms of knowledge and understanding about gases.

Further to this, students working beyond Grade 4 level will also:

- Explain the relationship between liquids and solids in terms of evaporation

- Make clear distinctions between the properties of solids, liquids and gases

- Explain why observations and measurements need to be repeated.

Check-up

Nappies are not the nicest smelling things, but part of real life and one that most students can relate to! The smell travels through the air to Aisha's nose, but hasn't reached her dad as he is further away. The water in the nappy evaporates once it is on the line to dry.

Assessment

WS 51

Use the Unit 5 assessment on WS 51 to check the students' understanding of the content of the Unit. The answers are given opposite.

Name: _____   Date: _____

WS 51   Unit 5 assessment

1 For each property write the state of matter it describes – **solid**, **liquid** or **gas**.
   a) Keeps its shape and its volume _____
   b) Flows but keeps its volume _____
   c) Easily squashed _____
   d) Evaporates _____

2 Hamid and Yasmin drew a line around a puddle. They wanted to see how it changed through the day.
   a) What two measurements could they take?
   _____
   _____
   b) How will the puddle change? _____
   _____
   c) Why will it change? _____
   _____

3 Name the gases that are:
   a) Essential for burning, respiration and life _____
   b) Essential for photosynthesis, puts out fires and found in fizzy drinks
   c) Put in 'lighter-than-air' balloons _____

Unit 5: Gases around us   51

Answers

1   a   Solid

    b   Liquid

    c   Gas

    d   Liquid

2   a   Distance across the puddle. Distance round the puddle.

    b   It will become smaller.

    c   Because water has evaporated from the puddle.

3   a   Oxygen

    b   Carbon dioxide

    c   Helium

The answer!

Refer back to the introductory question. House bricks are solid. But they have small spaces all through them and air is trapped in these spaces. When you put a brick in water, the water drives out the air and it rises as bubbles. So when you see a bubble, you are seeing air – or at least the space it takes in water!

Create an even more spectacular effect by putting a brick in a bucket on its end. Air bubbles will stream out. Now invert the brick. Air driven through it by water falling through the brick will be released in a second bubble stream.

And finally...

Create a wall display showing the different states of matter and their properties. Divide the board into three and ask the students to provide statements for each state's property. If you can attach this to a board with pins or use a sticky board, jumble up the statements and let the students sort them out as part of revision.

Include sealed jars of substances that smell as part of a permanent display for students to test their friends.

New International Edition

Unit 6: Electricity

The objectives for this Unit are that students should be able to:

- Explain why some simple circuits will work and other will not

- Understand how a switch can be used to break a circuit and stop the flow of an electrical current

- Collect evidence from investigations and evaluate how good it is

- Use their evidence to explain what they found out.

SB p.75   *Science background*

We've all seen a film where the storm is raging overhead, the lightning strikes the conductor atop the tallest tower of the castle on the rock, the evil Doctor Frankenstein pulls at an enormous switch and, after a series of jolts, flashes and fizzes, the monster, suitably electrified, comes to life. If only primary science was like that! Students usually have high expectations of what they'll be producing in lessons on electricity and can be disappointed when instead of fashioning Frankenstein's monster all they manage to do is light a bulb.

It is far easier to show what electricity does than to explain what it is. Over the last 300 years or so, many scientific minds have attempted explanations; and most of them have given their name to one measurement or other – volts, ohms, watts, amperes, coulombs and even henrys!

In Grade 4 it is more appropriate for students to investigate what they can do with electricity: how to construct a simple circuit, what conducts electricity and what doesn't, how circuits can be altered to change the current, how to incorporate a switch into a circuit and where this might be useful.

Although students will have learned about electricity before, they may still hold some common misconceptions, e.g. electricity travels from both ends of a battery and clashes at the component; batteries are 'full' of electricity which gets 'used up'; electricity can leak out of a cut wire; and electricity in a circuit becomes weaker on the other side of the component.

Language

Battery	Strictly, the collective noun for more than one cell; commonly used to mean 'cell' too.
Cell	A device that converts chemical to electrical energy.
Circuit	A closed path of conductors through which an electric current can flow.
Current	The flow rate of electrical charge. (The current is equal to the amount of charge passing a particular point per second. It is measured in amperes.)
Electrical conductor	A material that allows electricity to pass through it easily.
Electrical insulator	A material that does not allow electricity to pass through it easily.
Electron	Negatively charged particle moving around the centre of an atom.
Resistance	A measure of the difficulty of the flow of electrical current through a material; measured in ohms.
Series circuit	An electrical circuit that provides only one path for the electric current to flow.
Static electricity	The build-up of electrical charge in one place.
Switch	A device that can be used to control or stop the flow of an electrical current.
V	The symbol for volt.
Voltage	The amount of energy available to move charges from one point to another in a circuit; measured in volts.

The Words to learn list on page 75 of the *Student Book* can be used to make a classroom display.

Resources

- *Circuits and Conductors* Reader

- Selection of crocodile clips, bulbs, bulb holders, wires (of varying thickness)

- Selection of batteries

- Hand lenses

- Selection of household and home-made switches

- Samples of electrical conductors

- Samples of electrical insulators.

Bright ideas

- Inexpensive battery-powered toys from discount stores and markets provide good sources of electrical circuits in action. Allow students to explore the circuits to find out how they are connected, then to use the components in their own model-making.

Knowledge check

- Students should know the names of devices commonly used in simple circuits and appliances at home and in school, which use either mains electricity or batteries.

- Students should understand that an electrical device will not work unless there is a complete circuit and that a circuit needs a source of electricity.

- Students should know that some materials conduct electricity and that others do not.

- Switches can be used to break a circuit and stop the flow of an electrical current.

- Students should realize that in some situations electricity can be extremely dangerous.

⚠️ Warn students that they must never stick anything into a mains socket other than a plug and must never play around pylons or electricity substations. All school investigations are into low-voltage 'battery' current. Students must NEVER investigate mains electricity. Although safety warnings about the dangers of electricity are very important, the batteries and voltages you will be working with in school should not injure a student or produce an electric shock of any significance.

Skills check

Students need to:

- make careful observations and measurements

- collect evidence and decide how good it is

- use their evidence to explain what they found out.

Some students will:

- be able to explain how they matched different components for a particular circuit and describe what may happen if the components are not matched.

Links to other subjects

Literacy: Collecting information from a variety of sources and presenting it in one simple format, e.g. labelled diagram. Scanning texts on screen to locate keywords to use as a tool for summarizing text.

Numeracy: Measuring and comparing, using standard units. Organizing and interpreting simple data in Venn diagrams and tables.

ICT: Using multimedia packages to combine text and graphics to make a presentation. Using spreadsheets to record and analyse data. Using a light sensor.

Design and technology: Making switches and devices. Incorporating electrical components to operate lights, buzzers or motors.

Let's find out...

The Unit opens with this question:

Has your home got a hallway? Maybe there is a light on the landing. You can switch it on from the bottom of the stairs – and switch it off when you get to the top. One lamp, two switches and only one source of electricity. How can that work?

Homes with more than one floor – or flats accessed from a stairway – will have an electric light that can be lit from either ground or first floor level. This involves switches at both levels.

Tell the students they are going to find out about circuits and conductors. They will need some experience before they can meet this particular challenge.

101

Unit 6: Electricity – Simple circuits

The objectives for this lesson are that students should be able to:

- Understand that a complete circuit with a source of electricity is needed for a device to work

- Learn about how batteries work

- Build, draw and label their own batteries

- Find out that some materials conduct electricity and other do not.

SB pp.76–77

Starter

- Display a photograph of a building being struck by lightning. *Have any of you been caught out in a thunderstorm? What is lightning? Do you know how to keep safe if you are caught outside in a lightning storm?* (They should keep as close to the ground as flat as possible – never shelter under a tree.)

- Explain that the students are going to learn all about how electricity works.

Explain

It's electrifying!

Electrical charges are nothing new but it's only in the relatively recent past that we've been able to generate and control current electricity. Electricity that moves is called current electricity. The movement of negatively charged electrons in the atoms of a conducting material causes the electric current to flow. It's this stream of moving electrons that creates the current.

Demonstrate the stream of moving electrons with a quick game of pass the parcel with a difference – everyone sits in a circle, everyone has a parcel which must be passed at the same time. All the parcels should move simultaneously, just like electrons in the electric current. The electrons are already in the circuit. They are not 'created' by the battery or stored there.

Round and round

For electricity to flow it must be able to follow an unbroken path or circuit.

Ask the students to form a circle and hold hands. Squeeze the left hand of the student on your right.

When the student feels their left hand squeezed, they squeeze the hand of the next student in the circle and so on until the pulse comes back to the beginning. If anyone breaks the circle, then the pulse cannot get around. Explain that an electrical circuit works in the same way, only millions of times faster – if the circuit is broken, the electricity won't flow.

Making it work

Battery power is produced by a chemical reaction in the battery itself. A 'flat' battery is one in which the chemicals have been depleted. The current from a battery actually flows from negative to positive terminals though it may still be conventionally shown in diagrams as moving from the positive to negative.

> ⚠ Do not keep flat batteries as harmful chemicals can leak out of the casing. Never try to cut open a battery.

Things to do

Build a battery

Build a modern version of Volta's first battery described on page 77 of the *Student Book*.

A tube from chocolate sweets accommodates small coins well – these are the copper discs. The current produced is very small – not enough to light a bulb. However, you can 'hear' the electricity if you touch one of the wires to the plug end of a set of personal headphones and then scrape the end of the other wire onto the side of the plug. The crackling is the electricity from your battery.

Record

Students should draw their batteries and mark on the direction the current flows.

Support

Where has the electricity come from? Was there electricity in the coins or the salty water?

Building their own batteries will help students to understand how batteries provide a chemical 'push' to enable electricity to flow.

Extend

Make a tongue-tingling battery by inserting a copper coin and a galvanized (zinc-covered) nail into small slits in a lemon, about 1 cm apart. Clip wires to your metals and carefully put the bare ends on your tongue. You should feel a buzzing and tingling sensation – a tiny electric current.

Baffling batteries

Ask the students to look out for battery-powered things around them. They may forget the very small ones in watches and digital timers.

Record

Ask the students to record their discoveries. Where it is safe to look, ask them to record the voltages on the batteries. They will find that most are multiples of 1.5: such as 3, 4.5 or 9.

Support

Ask students to group the batteries by shape – cylinders, boxes or buttons.

> ⚠ Tell the students not to put button batteries in their mouths.

Extend

What can be powered by either battery or mains power? Radios are a common example. *Where are rechargeable batteries in use?* – in some torches, hand tools, and portable computers. *Why have they been chosen for this task?* You might come across some devices – especially torches – powered by hand squeezes. *What is going on there? And how can you have a clockwork radio?* These are questions to be answered later.

I wonder...

Fibreglass is an insulator and so provides some protection against accidental electric shock.

Electricians often use wooden ladders to prevent the current going 'to earth' through their bodies.

Dig deeper

Using textbooks and the Internet, find out about the life and work of Michael Faraday, one of the great electricity pioneers.

Did you know?

This is an opportunity to remind students that electricity from small batteries is safe, but mains electricity is dangerous.

Other ideas

Battery or mains?

Ask the students to think of a room in a house. *Which appliances use battery power and which use mains?* Some things may use both. *What sort of appliances use mains power – why do you think they don't use batteries? What are the advantages of battery power over mains?* Encourage the students to make a list of all the things they wouldn't be able to do if there was a power cut.

Counting the cost

Encourage students to think of ways to cut down on the amount of electricity they use. Let them design a poster urging people not to waste electricity.

ICT

Which room in a house has most electrical equipment? Use a spreadsheet to chart the results. Plot the results on a bar chart. *Are the rooms with most appliances used the most?*

Presentation

Design and make a poster to warn of the dangers of electricity when used incorrectly.

At home

Ask the students to find out where their electricity meter is at home. *How much electricity does your household use in a week?*

Plenary

How many other ways do we use electricity? See if the class can find 100 ways.

Unit 6: Electricity – Investigating circuits

The objectives for this lesson are that students should be able to:

- Investigate how to make a bulb light up

- Plan their own scientific investigation and predict what the results might be

- Record their results in a table and diagram

- Evaluate their investigations to consider what they could improve.

SB pp.78–79

Starter

- Hold up a small light bulb and display a photograph of a lit light bulb (or point to the real thing). *What do we need to do to get from this* (unlit bulb) *to this* (lit bulb)? Elicit students' understanding that a source of electricity is needed and that the bulb needs to be linked to the source in some way. *Should it be mains or battery electricity? Why?*

The challenge

Read the cartoon on page 78 of the *Student Book* and discuss the ideas about how to make the bulb light up. *Do you agree with them or not?* This is a good opportunity to assess some of the students' preconceptions and/or faulty thinking about electricity. Record all of the students' ideas or questions about electrical circuits. Display them in a prominent place and, as the topic progresses and their knowledge increases, revisit your list; tick those ideas which have proved true and cross out the incorrect ones.

What to do

Before you begin any practical work, ask the students to name all of the possible things that could go wrong in a circuit and cause the bulb not to light, e.g. flat battery, broken wire, loose connection, blown bulb, etc. Remind the students that before they give up on a circuit they expect to work, they should double check that each of the items they've listed is working properly.

Give pairs of students enough materials to complete a working circuit and let them experiment. Can they light a bulb with just one wire?

What you need

- Hand lenses

- 1.5 V batteries

- Battery holders

- Bulbs

- Bulb holders

- Wires

- Selection of household light bulbs

If you are short of materials, it's worth remembering that it is possible to make a functioning circuit with just a battery, a bulb and a strip of aluminium foil. Although battery holders, bulb holders and wires with crocodile clips do make our lives easier, you can get perfectly acceptable results with less expensive materials.

What to check

Are all of your components working properly? By replacing each one systematically you should be able to detect any broken pieces.

Students often believe that bulbs are not conductors because they associate a bulb with the glass globe rather than the tungsten filament. Make sure they are aware of the path of electricity through the bulb.

Support

Ask the students to look carefully at an unlit bulb through a hand lens. *Can you see the path the electricity could take?* They should notice that the electricity enters the bulb at one point, travels through the wire in the globe where it heats the wire so it glows and then leaves by a different point. It is travelling through metal all the time. *Why is that essential?*

Extend

Draw the unlit bulb and mark on it the path the electricity takes. Invite the students to look at a selection of light bulbs. *Can you see where the terminals are?* Terminals on a torch or MES bulb are the 'pip' on the base and the metal screw. This is also true of domestic Edison screw bulbs. Bayonet domestic light bulbs have two terminals – both on the base. Ask students to look for the terminals on other bulbs, e.g. car bulbs, tubular 'festoon' bulbs and LEDs.

What did you find?

Record

Students should record their results in a table. Students could also draw their finished, working circuit. Don't worry about students using conventional electrical symbols and circuit notation at this stage, although you will need to introduce them later on.

Present

Encourage the students to generalize from their results. They should find that the only circuits that worked were those that made a complete and unbroken path for the electricity to travel through. If there were any gaps, the current wouldn't flow.

Use a PowerPoint presentation to explain why some circuits worked and some didn't.

Can you do better?

WS 52

Would the students approach this investigation differently if they were asked to do it again? How good are the diagrams they've drawn? Could a friend make a circuit from their drawing?

Read the report on WS 52 with the students. *Do you think it was a fair experiment? What do you think about the conclusions? What would you have done better?*

Now predict

Two cells together should be joined from positive to negative terminals otherwise the cells do not work together and the circuit will not be complete.

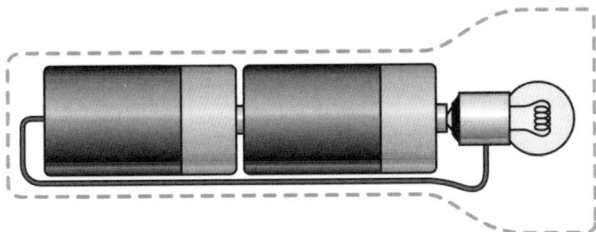

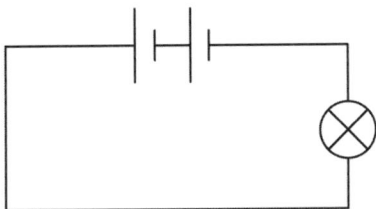

Note that this is not the same as 'jump-starting' a car. Here, the second battery replaces the first and so is connected positive to positive, negative to negative.

Other ideas

Quiz questions

Invite the students to design a quiz board with electrical questions and answers. The question and correct answer should be joined behind the board by insulated wires. They could link these with wires attached to paper clips or paper fasteners behind the board so that they can be moved around. Invite them to touch the question clip with a wire in a circuit linked to a buzzer; if they touch the right answer with the other wire then the buzzer will sound.

You can make lots of different quiz cards to support any subject. Muddle up the answers for the quiz to work.

ICT

Students often have difficulty producing clear drawings of electrical circuits. A drawing program could be useful here, especially if you are introducing the conventional symbols. Draw symbols for bulbs, batteries, motors and buzzers and copy them to disc. Students can then use these to prepare their own circuit diagrams.

At home

WS 53

Ask the students to find out about more bayonet and screw-fitting bulbs. They should draw the path of electricity through both. Emphasize that they must not remove bulbs from sockets.

Ask the students to complete WS 53.

Plenary

Play electricity 'beetle'. Give each component a number. The object of the game is to throw enough numbers on the dice to collect your components and make a complete circuit. It's up to you to decide on the complexity of the circuit.

105

New International Edition

Unit 6: Electricity – Conductors and insulators

The objectives for this lesson are that students should be able to:

- Understand that not all materials conduct electricity

- Find out which materials conduct electricity well

- Present facts on how to handle electricity safely

- Discover what an electrical insulator is and name some.

SB pp.80–81   Starter

- Display a photograph of a plug and socket. *Which materials in the photograph conduct electricity and which are insulators? Why is this important?*

- Prepare a circuit with a battery and bulb but use parcel string instead of wires (put crocodile clips on the ends for extra effect!). *Why doesn't this work?*

The challenge

Read the cartoon on page 80 in the *Student Book*. Discuss why Omar asked Layla to move. *Why was he so concerned?* We know that electricity flows through the wires in a circuit and the wires in a bulb. *Does it flow through every metal? Does it flow through other materials? How can we find out?*

What to do

Give the students a group of materials, both electrical conductors and insulators. Ask them to predict which will conduct electricity and which will not.

By inserting their material into the circuit they can test the material for conductivity.

What you need

- A selection of materials to test – both conductors and insulators

- Enough batteries, wires and bulbs to make a complete circuit for each pair or group

- Pencils that have been sharpened at both ends to reveal the 'lead' or carbon/graphite conducting rods

- Saturated salt solution.

What to check

The students need to decide on whether size is important. *Does it matter that the objects you choose to test are different shapes? If not, why not?*

All students should realize that metals make good conductors but most non-metals do not – carbon is the exception, conducting electricity poorly.

Support

Discuss how to make the test fair. Only one variable should be changed, i.e. the material. Everything else should be the same. The students shouldn't add more bulbs or buzzers.

Extend

Water can increase the conductivity of materials – including our bodies! Students should not handle mains electricity devices when wet. They could, however, experiment with the conductivity of water. Pure distilled water is an insulator. However, electricity can travel through water if it has salts dissolved in it. Although it doesn't always work very well, you can demonstrate it. Prepare a small volume of saturated salt solution and use two or three batteries to give you sufficient voltage. If your bulb doesn't light, move the wires in the water closer together.

Explain that the huge push of mains electricity can send a shock through the human body. Warn students that a human body wet from the bath is an even better conductor.

What did you find?   WS 54

Record

The students could record their results in a two-column table or a Venn diagram on WS 54.

Present

Keep one of the materials testers out on display for students to use. Can students find any other examples of conductors and insulators that you haven't thought about?

Ask the students to imagine that they work for an electricity company. Using a word processing or publishing program, encourage them to design a leaflet giving advice about the safe use of electricity in homes. They could include a 'spot the hazards' picture, as well as tips for electrical safety such as 'always replace worn cables', 'never touch a switch with wet hands', 'switch off the current before changing a light bulb', etc.

Can you do better?

WS 55

Ask students to complete the table on WS 55. *How can we generalize about electrical conductors and insulators?* Pencil 'lead' (graphite) is a poor conductor. It resists the flow of electricity and so dims the bulb. The more 'lead', the dimmer the bulb will be. There are conductors and insulators, but there are also 'poor conductors' like graphite.

Now predict

Discuss the result of the graphite test in Can you do better?. Explain that most non-metals do not conduct electricity very well but that carbon/graphite is a conductor. It's not as good as the copper wires we usually use however. Did the students notice anything that might suggest that?

Students will see that the bulb is less bright with a carbon/graphite conductor. The carbon offers a higher resistance to the current than metal does.

All materials conduct electricity to some extent but most non-metals have such high resistance that the current they can carry is negligible. If the voltage is high enough, however, even air, which is a good insulator, will allow electricity to pass

through it. Electricity at a high voltage can 'jump' from a power line to a kite string, a fishing rod, a yacht mast or a student's body.

Electricity travels through overhead cables at 44 000 V. Although carbon is not as good a conductor as metal, such a high voltage would have fatal consequences if it ran to Earth through a fishing rod. Use this as an opportunity to remind students how to stay safe around electricity.

Other ideas

Liar, liar

Wet skin conducts electricity better than dry skin so remind students that they should not operate electrical switches with wet hands.

Use this fact to make a spoof lie detector. Hook up an ammeter to your circuit and touch electrodes to your victim's skin! When your victim tells lies, the skin resistance goes down and the current goes up. *Can you work out why?*

At home

WS 56

Ask the students to make a list of the places in their home where they can find electrical insulators.

Ask the students to complete WS 56.

Plenary

Remind students of the predictions they made before they started their enquiry. *Were they correct?*

The best metal for conducting electricity is gold. *Why, then, do we use copper wires in our homes and not gold?*

Unit 6: Electricity – Designing switches

The objectives for this lesson are that students should be able to:

- Design a switch to operate components in a circuit

- Evaluate how successful their switch was

- Consider what they could do to improve their switches.

SB pp.82–83

Starter

- Demonstrate how to make a paper clip switch with a paper clip and two push pins and explain that when the paper clip touches the pins, the circuit is completed and electricity can flow through the circuit. Point out that all switches work in this kind of way – by making or breaking a circuit.

- Let the students make a very simple switch of their own. This could either be a paper-clip switch or a pressure switch using a piece of folded card with aluminium foil contacts.

The challenge

Read the challenge on page 82 of the *Student Book* and discuss the way Omar has decided to use a switch in his invention to set off an alarm. Do the students understand how this could work? *Have you any other ideas about how to make a rain detector?* One idea is to use sugar crystals in a clothes peg. Cover each jaw of the peg with foil, secure a wire to each one with a drawing pin and keep the jaws apart with sugar crystals – or a cube. As the rain dissolves the sugar, the peg closes and the jaws touch and complete the circuit.

What to do

Give the students time to discuss ideas for their inventions. Make sure they draw their circuits before trying to make them.

Encourage them to think of simple ideas with few moving parts. Generally, the simpler the switch the more effective it will be and the greater the satisfaction the students will have in seeing their invention work.

What you need

- A selection of electrical components

- A selection of electrical conducting materials

- Junk modelling materials

- Joining materials – glues, staples, tapes, etc.

What to check

What is the purpose of the circuit and will the switch work? Have the students thought carefully about what will make and break their circuit? *Is it the right circuit for the job?*

Support

Encourage the students to incorporate a very simple switch into a design – something like a pressure pad is a good example of a switch that is satisfying to make, yet straightforward to design. See page 83 of the *Student Book*.

Extend

Let the students consider using a more complicated switch such as a reed switch. Reed switches contain two thin metal strips in a strong glass tube. Bringing a magnet close to the switch draws the strips together and the circuit is closed. If you mount a magnet on a wheel so that it passes a reed switch as it turns, you can create a device for making a light flash on and off, as in a lighthouse.

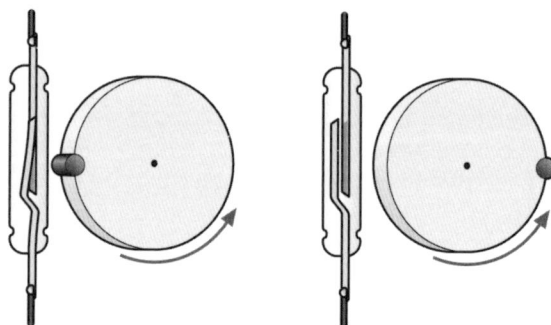

⚠ Reed switches are enclosed in thick glass but must still be handled with care.

What did you find?

If the students have built a rain detector, all they need to do is get out a watering can and see if it works. It's pretty much the same for the other designs students may have come up with.

Record

Encourage the students to write about the purpose of their design and why they chose the type of switch they did.

Present

Display design drawings alongside the finished models and allow each group to demonstrate their switches. Students could use a PowerPoint presentation to explain why their switch works and why they think it is a good design. Encourage constructive criticism of all designs.

Can you do better? [WS 57]

Can the students improve on their designs? *If you were starting again would you do things differently? What would you change and for what reason? What have you learned from each other?*

Read WS 57 with the students. *Do you think the thinking behind this design is sound? Explain why. Do you think it is a good design?*

Now predict

Safi needs some sort of alarm that is triggered when the light drops to a certain level. Students can make a control system to measure the light levels and power an alarm. To do this, they need control technology and a light sensor connected to the computer. You can also buy light-sensitive switches.

Other ideas [WS 58]

Junk modelling

A topic on electricity and switches affords endless opportunity for modelling – particularly if you can link this in with design and technology, as incorporating switches into models does take up a lot of time. Here are a few ideas that you could try:

* motorized buggies
* fairground roundabouts
* flashing birthday cards
* haunted house
* dlashing robot
* helicopter.

Use WS 58 to make and operate a morse code sender switch.

ICT

Let students investigate other applications of control technology to activate switches, e.g. use a temperature sensor to switch on a fan when the room gets too hot.

At home [WS 59]

Ask the students to count up the number of switches they can find in their home. *Which room has the most switches? Is that the room you spend most time in? Did you find any unusual switches? What were they?*

Ask the students to complete WS 59.

Plenary

Allow students time to present their work to the class and to describe how their switches work. *Who has been looking out for switches? What was the most interesting switch you found?* For example, there is one to turn off the fridge light when the door is shut; some shops have switches on their door to indicate that there is a customer in the shop; there are switches that open garage doors as the car approaches or that lift car park barriers.

Unit 6: Electricity – Brighter bulbs

The objectives for this lesson are that students should be able to:

- Explain how to change the brightness of bulbs, the speed of a motor or the volume of a buzzer in a circuit
- Plan and carry out a fair test
- Present their findings using graphs and ICT
- Find out what the wires in a plug look like and what the differently coloured wires do.

Starter
SB pp.84–85

- *Who has an electric toy? Who can switch it on and off? Who can make it go fast and slow?*

The challenge

Read the challenge on page 84 of the *Student Book* and discuss the students' ideas. *Do you agree with Zafar's friend's ideas? If not, why not?* Which do the students think is the most likely solution?

What to do

Decide on how to organize the test. *Is everyone going to test the same thing?* If you have a light sensor, you could use it to record brightness accurately. If not, cover each bulb with pieces of tissue paper until you can no longer see the filament glowing. The more pieces of tissue needed to mask the light, the brighter the bulb. This will give a more easily quantifiable result that can be graphed, rather than trying to describe the brightness in words.

What you need

- Batteries (and holders)
- A selection of wires
- Bulbs (and holders)
- Buzzers – buzzers are polarized: the red wire must go to the positive terminal of the battery, the black to the negative terminal. If your buzzer doesn't work, reverse the connections.
- A light sensor (optional)
- Tissue paper or tracing paper
- Electric motors.

What to check

The students should make Zafar's circuit to begin with and then decide how they are going to change one aspect of it.

Support

Make sure that the students are only changing and measuring one thing. Demonstrate a circuit with very bright bulbs. What do the students think will happen here if you add another battery? Point out that components are designed to be used at a particular voltage and if this is exceeded they will burn out.

Extend

Most students should recognize that adding batteries will make the bulbs brighter and that adding more bulbs to a circuit will make the bulbs dimmer. To extend this, set the challenge of adding bulbs to a circuit but keeping them equally as bright as before, i.e. introducing parallel circuits. In parallel circuits, each component has its own electric path, so that, e.g. the failure of one headlamp does not put out both of them.

What did you find?   WS 60

Record

The students could record their data in a table or on WS 60, then transfer this data and create bar charts or line graphs. As a fallback, they could use Zafar's results in the *Student Book*. 'Number of bulbs' should be on the x-axis and 'brightness of the light' on the y-axis. The numbers on the y-axis are arbitrary.

Present

Encourage the students to compile a PowerPoint presentation to show what they did in their investigation and to 'tell the story' of the graph. *When were the bulbs brightest or dimmest? Did the bulbs all have equal brightness?*

Can you do better?   WS 61

Ask the students how good their evidence was. *How could you tackle the investigation differently if you were starting again?*

Look at WS 61 and discuss it with the students. What conclusions have they drawn? Could they have done anything better?

Now predict

Look for an understanding that Zafar needs to incorporate a switch into her circuit. More able students may realize that by incorporating the buzzer and switch in a separate (parallel) circuit, Zafar can keep the headlights constantly bright whether she is using the buzzer or not. Let the students try to build a circuit that does just that.

Other ideas

Don't blow your fuse!

If you use a 1.5 V bulb with a 3 V battery, the bulb won't have a very long life; the filament will overheat and burn out. Similarly, if your domestic appliances carry too large a current through them, they can be damaged.

The working part of a fuse is the fuse wire; these wires can carry different currents and are made in different thicknesses. Fuse wires are made from metals with a low melting point (generally tin-coated copper). If too much current passes through the fuse the wire heats up and will eventually melt. When this happens the circuit is broken and this stops the flow of electricity.

Model a fuse with strands from wire wool. Over a tin tray, touch the end of the strand with wires from battery terminals; the strand will flare up and burn out!

ICT

Information from this activity could be entered into a graphing program and used to draw different types of graphs. Remind students that all axes should have labels and that their graphs should all have titles.

If you have one, let the students use a light sensor program to find which bulb in school is the brightest. *How do light bulbs compare to fluorescent lights or to candles or to the Sun?*

At home

WS 62

Tell the students that there are three different wires in a domestic plug: the live cable (which is brown), the neutral (blue) and the earth (green and yellow stripes). Show them what a plug looks like inside. Explain that the live and neutral wires carry the current and the earth wire is for safety. Old plugs had different coloured wires. Can the students find out what these colours were and why they were changed? Ask students to count, without touching, the plugs at home. How many are there?

> ⚠ Remind students that they should not take a plug apart.

Ask the students to complete WS 62.

Plenary

Computers are frequently used as switches. Quite apart from technological applications, students can explore their use with simple switch programs and logic gates. There are a number of commercial examples on the market which can be used to control electrical devices of all kinds. A common application is the programmable floor turtle; here switches determine the path taken by the toy. Use a floor turtle to demonstrate this.

Unit 6: Electricity – Magnets and metals

The objectives for this lesson are that students should be able to:

- Experience forces between magnets

- Discover that magnets can both attract and repel each other

- Find that magnets attract some, but not all metals.

SB pp.86–87

Starter

Put a strong magnet in your pocket – not close to a watch or any card with a black magnetic stripe if you hope to use it again! Press a magnetic object – a steel pencil or a pair of scissors, for example – against the pocket, so that it stays there.

Ask students what is going on. Why is this object 'stuck to you'? How can you get it off? Why does it jump back when you bring it close to your pocket?

Explain

An invisible force/magnetic metals

Students will have experienced magnets before. They should have explored them in Grade 3 in Magnets and Springs. This Unit revises and extends their understanding.

Magnets have the power to move things without touching them. They draw some metals to them. They repel other magnets.

All iron bars are made up of tiny particles. These particles are grouped together. Each little group or domain is a mini-magnet. Each mini-magnet pushes and pulls – all the time – like people in crowded in a lift facing in all directions and shoving each other around. Because they pull and push in every direction, the mini-magnets in an iron bar push and pull each other. But in a magnet, the mini-magnets all face one way and work together.

The mini-magnets at the ends of the bar face the open air. The mini-magnets grouped at one end can push. The mini-magnets grouped at the other can pull. So the magnetic forces in a bar magnet are concentrated at the powerful ends. We call these ends the magnet's poles. Every magnet has a

north pole and a south pole. Like poles repel each other; unlike pole attract.

Things to do

Push and pull

Ensure that students understand the meaning of the words attract and repel by 'pairing'. Each time you use the word, pair it with a short definition, and even hand movements. 'Attract – pull together'. 'Repel – push apart'.

Magnets can push and pull things without touching. There is a force field around each magnet. In this invisible field, the magnet can attract and repel some metal objects and other magnets. A piece of magnetic metal in the force field of a magnet is drawn to it. Bring another magnet into this force field and it may be attracted and trapped. But it may be repelled, so that you have to push hard to get the magnets to touch each other.

You know that a metal bar is a magnet is when it is repelled by another magnet.

Metal testing

All the common magnetic materials are metals, but the majority of metals are not noticeably magnetic. Iron, and its products like steel, are easily attracted. And so are some rarer metals like nickel and cobalt. The test of whether a metal object is a magnet itself is whether it repels another magnet. Only magnets repel each other. Small changes to metals can make them magnetic or non-magnetic. Steel is an alloy of iron, and it is magnetic. Steel is iron with a tiny amount of carbon and other chemicals in it. But stainless steel – which has a tiny amount of chromium in it too – is not magnetic. So it can be separated from ordinary steel in a scrap yard, using a magnet.

DO NOT test electrical devices, watches or cards with black strips!

Dig deeper

Electricity plus magnetism produces movement. And movement plus magnetism will produce electricity. If electricity flows through a wire, it produces magnetism and can move a magnet. And the reverse is true. If you move a magnet near a wire, then you generate electricity. Electricity generators contain magnets. When you make the magnets move – using a steam turbine, moving water or the power of the wind – you generate electricity.

I wonder...

Electromagnets have a wire coiled around a metal core. When the magnet is switched on, the coiled wire creates a magnetic field. When the electric current is turned off, an iron core will stop being an electromagnet, but a steel core becomes slightly magnetic.

Did you know?

- A magnetic field is invisible. It can work through some other objects. Put a magnet on the tabletop. The magnetic field works through the table.

- An electromagnet without electricity is just a metal bar in a coil of wire. But switch it on. It becomes a powerful magnet that can lift scrap metal, ring doorbells, or pull a steel splinter from your eye.

Other ideas

WS 63

How do you make a compass needle?

You need a strong magnet and a sewing needle, a cork and a bowl of water. Check that your needle is not a magnet. See if it attracts other needles. Then use your strongest magnet. Stroke the needle from one end to the other, using one pole of the magnet. Always use the same pole and stroke in the same direction. Try fifty strokes. Now see if you have made your needle into a magnet. Put the needle on a cork or a piece of polystyrene floating in a bowl of water. It should turn to face north/south.

Check your floating needle with a magnetic compass. What happens if you bring a magnet close to your floating needle?

How can you find the force field?

You need a bar magnet and a magnetic compass, a sheet of paper and a pencil. Put the bar magnet in the middle of the paper. Slide the compass close to it. Watch how the compass needle moves. Draw round the compass and lift it away. Now draw the way the needle was facing on the circle. Put the compass on the paper and draw the needle again - and again. Notice how the needles are facing. These directions are the magnets lines of force. Together, these lines make up the force field.

Which cans are magnetic?

Sort a collection of drinks cans into steel and aluminium, using a magnet. Test the ends as well as the sides - sometimes the ends of an aluminium can are made of steel. Cans are sometimes called 'tins' because the steel can is covered with a thin layer of tin. But tin metal is not magnetic - it is the steel inside that sticks to the magnet.

At home

Ask students to look around their home for examples of magnets in use. The fridge presents both fridge magnets and a magnetic strip that closes it. Then ask them to think of magnets as part of every electric motor. How many magnets are there now?

Plenary

For a fishing game, tie a magnet to one end of each thread. Tie the other end of the thread to the end of the stick to make a fishing rod. Cut some fish from paper, and slip a paper clip over each 'mouth'. Now see how many fish you and a friend can pick up with the magnetic rod. Who can catch the most?

Unit 6: Electricity – Unit 6 Review

The objectives for this lesson are that students should be able to:

- Check what they have learned about electricity in this Unit

- Find out how they are working towards, within and beyond the Grade 4 level.

SB
p.88

Expectations

Students working towards Grade 4 level will:

- Construct a simple working circuit

- Explain why some circuits work and others don't

- Recognize that a circuit needs a source of electricity

- Recognize that electricity can be dangerous.

In addition, students working within Grade 4 level will:

- Construct simple circuits and use them to test whether materials are electrical conductors or insulators and how switches work

- Recognize that voltage is the 'push' in the circuit

- Relate knowledge about metals and non-metals to their use in electrical appliances

- Describe how adding batteries affects the voltage in the circuit

- Systematically investigate the effect of changing components in a circuit on the brightness of bulbs.

Further to this, students working beyond Grade 4 level will also:

- Explain how they matched different components for a particular circuit, e.g. by voltage

- Describe what may happen if the components are not matched.

Check-up

In a circuit with two batteries, a bulb and a motor there are many things that could go wrong:

- one or other of the batteries could be flat

- the batteries could be joined the wrong way round

- the wires could be broken

- the wires could have an insecure connection to any of the other components

- the bulb could be blown

- the bulb and motor combined may require a greater current than the batteries can provide

- the components may not be matched.

Assessment

WS 64

Use the Unit 6 assessment on WS 64 to check students' understanding of the Unit. The answers are given opposite.

Answers

1 There should be a tick against copper coin and aluminium foil.

2 **a** A conductor

   b An insulator

3 Accept answers that indicate that the metal parts connect to the electricity supply and therefore need to be conductors and the plastic parts need to be insulators to protect us from electric shocks.

4 Circuit A because the switch is closed making a full circuit

The answer!

Refer back to the original question. To model an upstairs/downstairs light circuit, the electricity will need a path that is complete, whichever switch is used. So the electricity will need to flow to the light bulb through either switch – although they can share a common return wire to the battery. Either switch will complete the circuit; either will break it.

In reality, house wiring is more complex than that and lights may be on ring mains, which cannot easily be modelled.

And finally...

Complete the Unit by having an electricity quiz. Divide the students into teams. Each team needs to make a circuit with a switch, a buzzer and a light. When they know an answer to a question, they can close their switch to complete the circuit and make their buzzer buzz.

Unit 7: Sound

The objectives for this Unit are that students should be able to:

- Explore how sound travels as waves

- Understand that sound changes over distance

- Make careful observations and measurements in their investigations

- Make predictions and evaluate their evidence.

SB p.89 ## Science background

'In space no one can hear you scream!' was the slogan for the sci-fi horror film *Alien. Have you ever wondered if it's true?* When astronauts landed on the Moon they had to use radios to communicate with each other even though they were standing only centimetres apart. *Why?* Well, sounds are made when materials vibrate and can only travel through materials. Space is a vacuum and is a silent place because there is no air to carry sound vibrations. *Why could they communicate if they touched helmets?*

Sound travels as waves – vibrations of the material through which the sound travels. Sound waves travel in all directions in a compression wave; that is a wave made of 'pulses' of high and low pressure. When this pressure wave reaches us, our ears receive it and our brain converts the signals into something we recognize as a sound.

The height of the vibrations (called the amplitude) determines the loudness of the sound. Sound waves from an explosion or a jumbo jet are huge. Sound waves from a whisper are tiny. The number of vibrations each second (the frequency) determines the pitch of the sound – how high or low it is. Sound waves from a humming loudspeaker are very long. Sound waves from a flute are very short.

Sounds change with distance. If a school bell is rung, the students should notice that the bell is louder if they are standing further away. Sound emanates from a source and it travels out, up and down, spreading and dissipating as it goes. If it reaches your ear, you hear it.

As sound passes through an object, much of its energy is lost. Sound may be reflected from the surface of the object – closing the classroom door reflects the sound of the corridor. And sounds

are also reduced as they pass through the door. A soft, absorbent material is a very good insulator. It contains many air spaces and as the sound is transferred from material to air and back to material, its energy is reduced. This is why curtains deaden the sound in the room – they reflect very little and lose a lot in their folds and fibres. Insulating material like this makes good protective ear-muffs.

Students will have experienced the fall in sound level when they leave a busy classroom and the door is closed. *If sound travels through solid things, what is happening?* Some sound will pass through, but much is reflected. You will not hear the sounds on the other side. *But why do double-glazed windows work so well as sound stoppers?* The sound has to pass through several materials – air and glass. Many double-glazed windows enclose a vacuum. Without a medium for transmission, sound cannot pass. The only sounds you hear from inside this double-glazed window are transmitted through the frame.

Language

Decibel (dB)	Unit of measurement of how loud or quiet a sound is. Decibels are a logarithmic scale – so 20 dB is much more than twice as loud as 10 dB.
Echo	The reflection or bouncing back of sound waves from a surface.
Muffle	To deaden a sound or make it quieter.
Note	In music when a sound is made at a particular pitch.
Pitch	How high or low a sound is.
Sound wave	The regular pattern of vibrations that move through a material.
Source	The place where something originates.
Tension	How tightly something is stretched.
Tuning	The adjustment of musical instruments to accurate pitch.
Vibrate	Move a small distance backwards and forwards very quickly.
Volume	How loud or quiet a sound is.

The Words to learn list on page 89 of the *Student Book* can be used to make a classroom display.

Resources

- *Changing Sounds* Reader
- A selection of tuning forks
- Junk modelling materials
- Musical instruments – pitched and un-pitched
- Drums and drumsticks
- A stereo system or loudspeakers
- Balloons
- Elastic bands of varying lengths and widths
- Drinking straws
- A clock with audible tick or metronome
- Sandwich bags
- A selection of sound insulating materials, e.g. cotton wool, foam, bubble wrap, newspaper
- Glass bottles (e.g. milk bottles).

Bright ideas

Start collecting junk modelling materials early in the term and ask students to bring in boxes and bits and pieces from the list.

Knowledge check

- We hear sounds through our ears.
- Sounds are made when objects vibrate.
- Sound takes time to travel.
- Sound travels through materials. We can hear sound through solids, liquids and gases.
- We can change the sounds that are produced by musical instruments in different ways.
- Sounds can be high or low, loud or quiet.
- Sound travels better through solids than liquids – and better through liquids than gases.

> ⚠ Warn students that they must never put anything into their ears.

Skills check

Students need to:

- make careful observations and measurements
- collect evidence and decide how good it is
- use their evidence to explain what they found out

- suggest productive questions to investigate
- generalize from their results.

Some students will:

- be able to describe ways in which the pitch of a sound made by a particular instrument or vibrating object can be raised or lowered.

Links to other subjects

Literacy: Reading and following instructions. Recognizing and using onomatopoeia. Producing sound effects for a radio play.

Numeracy: Measuring and comparing using standard and non-standard units. Organizing and interpreting simple data in bar graphs and tables.

Music: Recognizing families of instruments, understanding how musical notes are produced and changed, appreciating dynamics in music and investigating musical scales, composition and notation.

ICT: Using multi-media packages to combine text and graphics to make a presentation. Using recording equipment. Using spreadsheets to record and analyse data. Using a sound sensor.

PSHE: Considering life as a person with a hearing impairment.

Geography: Investigating noise pollution and its effect upon our environment.

Let's find out...

The Unit opens with this question:

> *Tariq's brother bought him a drum kit for his birthday. Tariq is delighted and plays it every night. Tariq's mum is not so happy. She thinks it's far too noisy and is worried about disturbing the neighbours. She's told Tariq that if he can't make the drums quiet, the drum kit will have to go. What can he do?*

Discuss Tariq's problem and encourage the students to suggest solutions. *Can the sound of the drums be changed in any way or can Tariq change something else to stop the noise being heard?*

117

Unit 7: Sound – Making sounds

The objectives for this lesson are that students should be able to:

- Understand that sound always has a source and many things can make sounds

- Discover that sounds are made when objects vibrate

- Observe how sounds travel through solids, liquids and gases

- Use ICT to make a sound meter for recording sound levels in their school.

SB pp.90–91   Starter

- Display pictures of a skier and snowy mountains. Tell the story of a skier's narrow escape! Explain that she was skiing in the mountains and a loud sound caused an avalanche! The sound had made the air shake which had loosened the snow and caused it to move down the hillside.

Some students may have experienced sliding down a sand dune. As you slide, the sand grains vibrate together, producing a low hum.

Explain

Sound vibrations

Sound is energy we can hear. All sounds start with something that is vibrating. Clash a couple of big cymbals together. *What can you see?* Students should be able to see the edge of the cymbal vibrating. Explain that this fast movement is called a vibration and it's the basis of all sound. Touch the cymbal and the vibrations stop – so does the sound.

Spreading sounds

As sound passes through a sound conductor it closes the distance between particles. The particles bounce apart again – energy moves in a compression wave. Demonstrate this by stretching out a 'Slinky' toy. Push one end and see the waves of energy flow along Slinky's coil.

The students can imitate these waves in a line. At one end is the student who is the sound source; at the other, a student who is 'the ear'; the students in the middle are air particles. As the 'sound' begins, the first student gently pushes the second. When this 'air particle' receives the push, they gently push

the next student until all of the line is moving and the 'ear' feels a push and has heard the sound.

Sound spreads in all directions from its source – including up and down. The further away from the source, the fainter the sound will be. Go outside and quietly hit a drum. How far can students move away before they can no longer hear the beat? Now hit the drum harder – can they move further away?

Has the louder sound travelled further? Say that you'll stop beating the drum from time to time and they must stop when they can't hear it. This may help reduce the likelihood that some students will insist they can hear a silent drum!

Sound travels

Sound travels by making the particles it's travelling through vibrate in one direction. The sound of a tuning fork is easier to hear when it causes a solid to vibrate. Demonstrate how to strike a tuning fork correctly on a firm, but not hard, surface; rest its vibrating end on a solid surface to increase the volume of the note.

If you have a recording of whale music, play it to illustrate that sound can travel by vibration through liquids like water as well as through air.

Things to do

See the sound

All of these activities are designed to make sound vibrations visible.

Record

Students could draw pictures of what they think is happening to the air around the vibrating objects.

Support

Lay a hi-fi speaker flat and put some rice or small polystyrene balls in the middle of it. Play a CD and watch the balls bounce around. Ask the students to put their hands gently on the speaker. They should be able to feel the vibrations. When the music stops, so do the vibrations. Say that vibrations are like movements that make the air shake.

Extend

Ask students to use secondary sources to find out what an oscilloscope is (a device that displays the pattern of a sound wave on a screen). They may have seen versions of oscilloscopes on a CD or computer sound system where pulses of sound are translated into flashing lights.

Dig deeper

The volume of sound is measured in decibels (dB). The softest measurable sound is 1 dB, which is the sound of falling snow. A whisper is about 30 dB and quiet talking is about 50 dB. Loud rock music reaches 110 dB and a plane taking off as much as 140 dB.

I wonder...

We see lightning before thunder because sound travels at a much slower speed than light. The speed of light is about 300 000 kilometres per second compared with the much slower 335 metres per second of sound.

Did you know?

Sound cannot travel in the vacuum of space because there is nothing to pass on the vibrations of the sound wave. Sounds don't always reach your eardrums directly; sometimes the sound waves are diverted or interrupted, which is why your voice won't carry so far on a windy day.

Other ideas

WS 65

Speed of sound

Send a student to the furthest point of the school playground and ask them to drop a coloured flag and blow a whistle at exactly the same moment. *Did you see the flag drop or hear the whistle first?* As light travels far faster than sound, you should see the flag drop before the sound of the whistle reaches you. Students can use WS 65 to support their work.

Softly, softly

Students take turns to make very quiet sounds and the student who is 'it' has to point in the direction of the sound. *Whose ears have the best sense of direction?*

ICT ideas

Use a sound meter to record the sound level at different locations in your school. Make a sound map of the different levels of sound you find. *Is the library really the quietest place? Is the playground always noisy? Are the sound levels the same throughout the day or do they change?*

Presentation

Invite the students to make and present a survey of people's favourite sounds and the sounds they least like. Let them present their information as a pictogram or bar chart.

At home

WS 66

Ask the students to make a list of all the sounds they can hear at home during a ten minute interval. *Which sound is the loudest? Which is the quietest? Which sound has come from furthest away?*

Ask students to complete WS 66, which reviews their learning so far.

Plenary

Have a karaoke competition to see who can produce the most interesting sound or just try singing instead. Make a 'vibratometer' to use for scoring the levels of vibrations. Alternatively, let the students draw what they think the various vibrations look like on their white boards and hold them up after each act.

119

Unit 7: Sound – How sound travels

The objectives for this lesson are that students should be able to:

- Identify materials that sound travels through

- Carry out an investigation on which materials muffle sound

- Plan a fair test

- Evaluate their results and consider how to improve their investigations.

Starter
SB pp.92–93

- *How can we hear someone knocking on a door? He's not in the same room. What is the sound travelling through?*

- Ask the students to listen quietly for sounds they can hear coming from outside the classroom. *Where have they come from? What materials must they have travelled through to reach our ears?*

The challenge

Read the challenge on page 92 of the *Student Book* and discuss how the students could hear sounds but couldn't see the source of the sound. Remind students that sound travels by vibration. *Can things other than air vibrate?*

What to do

Use sandwich bags that have zip-locks along the top edge for a close seal; otherwise you'll end up with flour and water everywhere! This investigation works best if you only half-fill the bags and squeeze out the extra air.

If you don't have a suitable clock, the students can still complete the investigation by tapping with a coin on the table top as they put their ear on the bag. They'll get similar results.

What you need

- Any selection of materials will do; make sure you have a solid, a liquid and a gas

- Sandwich bags with seals

- A clock or watch with an audible tick.

What to check

The real challenge is how to keep a class of students quiet enough to hear a watch ticking! The students only have to be silent for a very short space of time.

Support

Students often cannot understand how sound travels through solid objects; they may believe that somehow 'particles' of sound creep through gaps in doors or windows. You might find that using the term 'passing on' is less confusing than 'passing through' for such students. Talk about how the vibrations are passed on from one substance to another.

Bone is a good sound conductor. Ask the students to tap a plastic ruler – they're hearing the sound through air. Now invite them to put the ruler between their teeth and tap again – they should hear a much louder sound as the bones transmit the sound directly. Ensure rulers are wiped clean before and after use.

Extend

All students should be able to distinguish that sound can travel through solids, liquids and gases to a greater or lesser degree.

Some students may realize that the best transfer of sound happens when the particles in the material are close together.

Others may realize that in this test they are never truly listening through air or water alone as the plastic bag (a solid) affects the sound transfer.

What did you find?
WS 67

Record

Students can use the table on WS 67 to record their results. Make sure that the students are clear about which material the sound had to travel through for them to be able to hear it. If the results are inconclusive, they could use the data for Jain and Sayed's results in the *Student Book*.

Present

Let each group of students present their findings. They should include their table of results and be encouraged to generalize from these results. The closer together the particles in a substance are, the better the sound transmission. The air-filled bag is likely to produce the quietest result as gases have the most spread out particles and so do not transmit sound as well as solids or liquids.

Can you do better?
WS 68

Introduce the students to the idea of a decibel as a unit for measuring how loud a sound is. Don't try and go into too much detail as it is a logarithmic scale.

Would the students approach this investigation differently if they were asked to do it again? Can they think of a way of doing this investigation without the plastic bag? Is there a more accurate way of recording volume using a sound sensor?

Ask students to complete WS 68.

Now predict

Moving your ear away from the plastic bag severs the link between the sounds travelling through the solid plastic to your ears. Sound doesn't travel as well through air and so the resulting sound should be quieter. Use this point to reinforce that as we get further away from the source of a sound it becomes quieter. Listening through a wall is aided by using a drinking glass. It makes a better connection to our ear!

Other ideas
WS 69

String telephone

Tell students to follow the instructions on WS 69 carefully. The string telephone using taut string between two paper cup ear/mouth pieces wouldn't work if sound couldn't travel through the solid string. The most effective telephones are those using nylon fishing line or wire. On a calm day the students should be able to transmit sounds along the string over a fair distance.

ICT ideas

If you have one, use a sound sensor to measure the sound levels through different materials on a bar chart and use a graphing program to help.

At home

Explain that some sounds are often too quiet for us to hear normally and that sometimes we need to hear only those sounds. A stethoscope is an instrument that picks up sound waves from our bodies and leads them directly to a doctor's ears. Ask the students to try to make a stethoscope to hear their heart beating. They should push a small funnel into each end of a plastic tube and hold one funnel over their heart and the other over their ear. They should hear their heart beating. If they don't have funnels they could make a cone from a sheet of card, put it onto a friend's chest and listen carefully, covering their other ear.

Plenary

The further away from a sound we are, the quieter it will be as the sound waves spread out and weaken as they move from the source. Listen again to the sounds in the classroom; now try to hear sounds inside school but from other places, e.g. students talking, the school bell, the ring of a telephone, etc. Remind students of the journey of the sound wave and what it's travelled through. Now listen for sounds from further away – traffic perhaps, a football match on the school field, dogs barking. *How far have they travelled to reach your ears?*

Unit 7: Sound – Muffling sound

The objectives for this lesson are that students should be able to:

- Find out which materials reflect sound better than others

- Find out which materials muffle sound better than others

- Consider why different materials are better for soundproofing

- Decide what evidence to collect.

Starter
SB pp.94–95

- Go into the classroom rubbing your eyes and yawning. Apologize to the students because you didn't get much sleep last night; next-door's baby was crying all night and their dog was barking. When you finally did get to sleep you were woken up by the roadworks outside. *What can I do to get a good night's sleep tonight?*

The challenge

Read the beginning of page 94 in the *Student Book*. Discuss why the sounds in Ali's empty room sounded different to when it was full of furniture. Take a walk through school. *Do your footsteps sound quiet on carpet? Do your steps sound loud in the empty school hall?*

Ask the students to think of a sound wave as a bouncy super ball – if you throw it forcefully into a room with hard, bare walls it will bounce around much more than if you threw it into a room full of soft cushions. This is the way sound behaves with hard and soft surfaces and why things sound louder in empty rooms. Discuss how some materials can reflect sound back at you (an echo) and others seem to absorb sound.

What to do

Divide the students into groups with the materials they'll need to make their soundproof box. Decide on how to organize the test. Is everyone going to test all of the materials? Encourage the students to work systematically through the samples and to record their results as they find them. Too often, students will want to get on with the testing and neglect the recording, and then they forget their results. Make sure that they have completed and

recorded each test before they move on to another sample.

What you need

- A clock or metronome with a regular ticking sound – you really need something with a loud tick or buzz as the card boxes themselves muffle quite a bit of sound

- A selection of materials to test, e.g. newspaper, felt, cotton wool, bubble wrap, polystyrene, foam

- Two boxes with lids – one box must fit inside the other with a gap large enough to be surrounded by soundproofing materials, e.g. a small shoebox and a photocopy paper box are ideal.

What to check

The students need to decide how they are going to measure the sound intensity. Using subjective methods is fine as long as the students all agree on what they are hearing. They might like to measure how far away they are from the box when they can no longer hear any ticking. Think about taking an average measurement for the group.

If you have one, a sound sensor will, of course, give you quantifiable readings.

Support

Discuss how to make the test fair. Only one variable should be changed, i.e. the packing material. Everything else should be the same. Decide on what you are going to measure and how.

Reinforce that the sound made inside the box is the same all the time; it only changes because of the journey it makes through the boxes and the packing.

Extend

Encourage students to look at materials that reflect or bounce sound.

What did you find?
WS 70

Record

The students can use the table on WS 70 to record their results or use Ali's data in the *Student Book*.

Present

Ask the students to pretend that they are product testers for a company making ear protectors for noisy industries. They should explain which material muffles sound the best and which could be used to make the most effective ear protectors.

Can you do better?
WS 71

Use WS 71 to plan an investigation of sound-proofing materials.

Ask students to review how good their evidence was. How would they tackle the investigation differently if they were starting again?

People who work around noisy machinery in factories, road building or on airstrips need to wear ear protection to muffle the noise. Exposure to very loud sound over a long period can result in hearing loss. Let the students find out what material real ear protectors are made from.

Soft materials absorb sound and stop the sound waves from reflecting. Theatres and cinemas often have thick carpeting on the floors and even on the walls to prevent echoes.

Now predict

Hands up who sings in the bath or the shower! The reason our voices sound better in these types of spaces is because hard materials, like bathroom tiles, reflect sound. Our voices echo around the small space of the bathroom and the natural amplification makes us all think we're pop stars!

The same effect will happen in the school gym. Although the bodies of the dancers will absorb some of the sound, loud music will travel through the walls. To reduce this, you should hang drapes around walls, doors and windows, which will help absorb the sound.

Other ideas
WS 72

Noise pollution

Who lives in the noisiest street? Unwanted sounds around us are sometimes called 'noise pollution' – things like aircraft or traffic noise, and noise from quarries or building work. Although many of the noises are created in a useful cause some, like barking dogs, shouting or loud music, may be considered to be just anti-social. Hold a debate on this topic – 'Should we be able to make as much noise as we like?'

Students could use WS 72 to investigate the noisiest place in the school.

ICT ideas

If you have one, use your sound sensor to measure the volume of sounds and how they change through different materials.

Use control technology and your sound sensor together to design a device that is sound activated – a light switch or burglar alarm, for instance.

At home
WS 73

The students may have a sound-activated toy that starts to move or speak when it detects sounds above a certain volume. Some lights and key rings also operate by sound activation. Ask the students to find out about sound-activated devices and to list as many as possible.

Ask students to complete WS 73, which models planning an investigation.

Plenary

Remind students of the ideas they had before they started their enquiry. *Were they correct?* Have the students learned anything that could help with your noise problem? *What could you do to make your sleep a little quieter?*

123

Unit 7: Sound – Pitch and volume

The objectives for this lesson are that students should be able to:

- Understand what volume and pitch mean and use them in their work

- Represent different sound waves in drawings

- Find out how the pitch of a string depends on its length and thickness

- Learn that the volume and pitch of an instrument can be changed.

SB pp.96–97

Starter

- Paint or cover three coffee jars so you cannot see inside them. Half fill each with exactly the same amount of water. Ask a student to drop a large lump of Plasticine into one of the jars, put the top on all of the jars and mix them up. Say you will be able to detect which jar the Plasticine is in without looking inside the jars or picking them up! Take a drumstick and strike each jar to make a note – the jar with the different note (lower) is the one with the Plasticine lump in it. *How did I do it?* The Plasticine raised the water level and changed the pitch of the note.

Explain

Different instruments and different materials make different sounds. A clarinet made from wood sounds different to one made from metal. Instrumental sounds can be changed in two main ways: pitch and volume.

Different sounds

Scientists often represent sounds as waves. The energy the sound wave carries determines how loud it is. This energy is called amplitude (or sometimes intensity) and is measured in decibels. The sound level can be increased by, e.g. blowing a trumpet harder; this increases the size of the vibrations and so increases the sound. Sounds of different amplitudes make waves of different heights.

A quiet sound looks like this:

A louder sound looks like this:

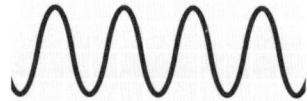

Give the students a range of musical instruments and encourage them to explore how the sounds are made. *Which part of the instrument is vibrating? Make the quietest sound you can, then make the loudest sound you can. What did you have to do?* Generally, the more energy they apply to making the sound, the louder it will be.

High or low?

Pitch is how high or low a sound is. Sounds of different pitches have different frequencies. Frequency is the number of waves passing a particular point in a second so it's the speed of the vibrations rather than the size that accounts for pitch. Different frequencies produce different notes. Sounds of different frequencies make waves of different speeds.

A high sound has the crests of the wave very close together and looks like this:

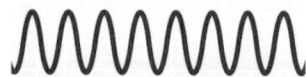

A low sound has a slower, more spread-out wave and looks like this:

Changing the length of the vibrating column of air in an instrument will change the pitch of the note produced. This applies equally to stringed instruments, woodwind, brass or any percussion instrument.

A short or small instrument vibrates quickly and produces high notes. Large or long instruments vibrate more slowly and produce lower pitched notes.

Tight strings or drum skins produce higher pitches than loose ones.

The lowest sung note in a classical composition is in Osmin's aria from 'II Seraglio' by Mozart; the highest is also in a Mozart piece, 'Papolo di Tessaglia'.

Things to do

Pitch-pipes

Straight plastic drinking straws are better than art straws for this as the ends don't go soggy.

Record

The students could try to draw what they think is happening to the sound wave as their pipes got shorter.

Support

Let the students practise getting a steady note before the straw is first cut. If this is too tricky, prepare several different sized straws for them to try. An alternative is to use a slide whistle, which has an adjustable tube inside that can be shortened or lengthened easily.

Extend

Encourage the students to investigate the mathematical relationship of the length of pipe to the note it produces. Pythagoras discovered that the notes on a musical scale have a mathematical relationship to each other:

Notes on scale	Do	Re	Me	Fa	So	La	Ti	Do
Their relationship	1	$\frac{8}{9}$	$\frac{4}{5}$	$\frac{3}{4}$	$\frac{2}{3}$	$\frac{3}{5}$	$\frac{8}{15}$	$\frac{1}{2}$

I wonder...

Both prey and predators need good ears. Prey animals like rabbits have large, mobile ears that they can turn, to detect an approaching enemy. Predators like cats and dogs have smaller, forward-facing ears that they move to help them to locate their prey. By moving their ears, they can better estimate the position and nature of a source of sound.

Dig deeper

Students could explore the more bizarre ways that animals produce sound.

Did you know?

Animals can hear a different range of sounds to humans. Sounds with a higher pitch than those that human ears can hear are called ultrasounds; those that are lower are called infrasound. The pitch of a sound is measured in hertz (Hz), which represents the number of vibrations per second: 1 Hz is one vibration per second.

Other ideas

Straw slide

Partly cut through a drinking straw and bend it at right angles to itself. Put the long end in a cup of water and gently blow through the short end to create a stream of air over the longer cut end. It you can't make it whistle, try pinching the top of the straw. Move the straw up and down in the water to change the pitch of the note.

Higher or lower?

Play a pitch identification game. In pairs, let the students blow notes on a recorder or hit them on a xylophone for a blindfolded friend. Can their friend identify which is the highest and lowest note? What if they used two different instruments?

Presentation

Invite the students to make a display of flying bats or whistling dolphins using paper cut-outs. Help them to compile a chart showing which animals have the best hearing.

At home

Ask the students to make a list of sounds in their house that signal something. They should think about sounds we hear as warnings such as emergency sirens. *Are they high or low pitched? Can you think why this might be?*

Plenary

Students often confuse volume and pitch. Ask them to sing (or play tuned percussion) louder, softer, higher and lower.

Unit 7: Sound – Changing pitch

The objectives for this lesson are that students should be able to:

- Find out how to change the pitch of a string
- Plan a fair test and decide what they will change and keep the same
- Record their results using ICT
- Plan and deliver a presentation on the history of sound and music.

SB pp.98–99

Starter

- Play a few excerpts from Benjamin Britten's 'Young Person's Guide to the Orchestra'. Can the students identify any of the instruments being played by their sound? *Which are the highest pitched? Which the lowest pitched?*

- If any of the students play an instrument, ask them to bring them in and play a tune for the class. Find a few examples of instruments for students to look at.

- Show a photo of a person playing a guitar. *How does the person playing it change the pitch of the notes he produces?*

The challenge

Read the challenge on page 98 of the *Student Book* and discuss what students know about the cello and oud. Review how the musicians talk about changing the pitch of their instruments to get high and low notes. Make sure the students have secure knowledge about the difference between describing pitch and volume.

What to do

The *Student Book* identifies three options. The students could do any or all of these. Decide on how to organize your groups and which variable each group is going to change. If you are looking at slightly different investigations, it's important to be clear about the experimental variable that will affect the pitch change – whether it is length, width or tension.

What you need

- Paper cups to act as amplifying sound boxes
- Strings (nylon kite string is good as it is uniform and strong but you could use other types)
- Clear sticky tape
- Rulers
- Paper clips
- A selection of elastic bands of different widths and lengths
- Margarine tubs or boxes to stretch your bands over
- A tape recorder or video camera
- Hanging masses or suspended cups to hold weights.

What to check

Make sure the students are clear about the variables they will change and what they will keep the same. How will the students record their sounds? It can be difficult to compare the pitch of an elastic band to the pitch of a tuned instrument, for example. It is often easier to compare the pitch of an elastic band with that of another similar band, e.g. *If I stretch this it will sound higher,* rather than to try and ascribe a value to it. Subjective observations like these make comparisons with others more problematic but do open up a subject for discussion.

What did you find?

Record

This should show that the shorter the string, the higher the note, the tighter the string, the higher the note and the thinner the string, the higher the note. So a long, fat, loose elastic band will have a lower twang than a short, thin, tight one.

Omar and Yasmin were shortening their string by a fixed amount each time but the pitch would not go up in even steps because of the mathematical relations of pitch described on page 125.

Present

The students should be able to make some graphic representation of the relationship between the two variables. They could present their findings using ICT.

Can you do better?
WS 74

The quality and the problems of quantifying evidence are good points for discussion here. Can the students think of a more scientific way of recording the differences in pitch of their strings? Could they use electronic pitch-pipes to try and match the sound they make?

Use WS 74 to model recording an investigation.

Now predict

In an orchestra the instruments are tuned to the pitch of the oboe. Tuning reflects the way in which the instrument makes a sound. Woodwind and brass instruments are tuned by slightly changing the length of the whole instrument. The musician adjusts the length of the vibrating column of air in an open position by extending the length of the instrument at the joints. In a stringed instrument the pitch is changed to be in tune with the other members of the section by tightening or loosening the tension of the strings. A percussionist changes the pitch of a drum by tightening or loosening the skin.

Other ideas

Carnival of the animals

Make your own version of Saint-Saens' 'Carnival of the Animals'. *Which sounds would you choose to represent birds or lions, snakes or seals?*

Record the music made. Invite the students to make a CD cover to go with it.

Old recordings

In the age of CDs and MP3, old vinyl records fascinate students. Time to get out your collection and give those old records a spin! American inventor Thomas Edison made the first sound recording in 1877; it was a recording of the nursery rhyme 'Mary had a Little Lamb'. He called his invention the phonograph. It was a cylinder covered in tin foil. Later, records were made from a plastic called vinyl. Pits and grooves were cut into the surface of a vinyl disc and, as a needle travelled through these grooves, it changed the vibrations into sounds we can hear. Records went round under the needle on a turntable. *What happens to a record's pitch when the turntable speeds up?*

Presentation

Invite the students to pretend that they are curators in a music museum and to make a time line of the history of music or the history of recording. Suggest that they illustrate their time line with pictures and have examples of music from different time periods on tape for people to listen to. Encourage them to predict what the music of the future might sound like. What instruments will we be playing in a hundred years' time?

At home
WS 75

Ask the students to research an interesting instrument, maybe from a different culture. Let them find out how the instrument produces sound, what it's made from and where it's used. *Is your instrument still popular today?*

Ask students to complete WS 75, which reviews their learning so far.

Plenary

Play some extracts from Saint-Saens' 'Carnival of the Animals'; 'Fossiles' (high notes) and 'L'éléphant' (low notes) show a good contrast of sounds. Talk to the students about the different instruments used to make the sounds which are high and low pitched and why.

Unit 7: Sound – Different instruments

The objectives for this lesson are that students should be able to:

- Discover how different instruments make different sounds

- Learn that a column of air in a wind instrument vibrates to make sound

- Find out how to alter the pitch of a wind instrument

- Evaluate and explain their results.

SB pp.100–101

Starter

- Finish off a packet of crisps. Now blow up the bag and explode it by punching it between your hands. *What made the noise?* The air, of course!

- Show a photo of a selection of wind instruments or bring in a selection of wind instruments. *What do these all have in common?*

Explain

Tubular tones

Many instruments, particularly in the orchestral woodwind and brass families, producing sound from air vibrating in a single tube. The length of the tubing can be altered either by using valves to increase or decrease the length of tube (or by manually moving a slide in and out, in the case of a trombone) or by covering up finger holes.

The shorter the tube, the higher the pitch of the note created when you blow into or over it. The longer the pipe, the lower the pitch of the note will be.

The width of the pipe also affects the pitch of the note it makes. Narrow tubes produce higher note than wide tubes.

This is exactly the same principle as with vibrating strings – except this time it's the air in the tube rather than a solid string which is vibrating.

Junk box band

In this revision activity, the students should be able to identify the parts of the instruments that vibrate and cause the sound. They might even try making some of these themselves.

The lolly stick twanger imitates a zither where the notes plucked vary with the length of the string. Here the 'string' is made from wood. You can get the same effect using plastic or wooden rulers clamped to a table and overhanging the edge by different lengths.

The pan pipes and kazoo both make different sounds as the length of the column of vibrating air is changed. A comb and paper work by air vibrating across the paper to produce a buzzing sound; the wobble board is similar with the air around the board being moved. Shakers make sounds as the loose objects inside move and produce vibrations. Drums and other percussion instruments make the air inside them vibrate when they are hit – different sized drums make different sounds. The bullroarer is just a tube that is swung around; as the air moves over the elastic band it causes it to vibrate.

Things to do

Bottle organ

This activity works in a similar way to the pan pipes scale. The Pythagorean scale works here as before, although this time, air blown across the top of the bottle causes the air inside the bottle to vibrate and make the sound. You don't have to use the traditional eight-note scale. Chinese music is sometimes based on a five-note scale and some Indian music uses a scale of 22 notes!

Ensure that the students understand how the sound is being made. Point out that, by changing the depth of the water, you are also changing the length of the column of air. Hitting the bottle organ with a stick instead of blowing across the top causes the bottle and the water to vibrate and a different sound and a different pitch is obtained.

Record

Let the students make the water in each of their bottles a different colour and measure the depth. They should also measure the length of the column of air. Show them how to make fraction strips to show the relationship of one to another and arrange them in an ascending scale.

Support

It's not necessary to make a whole octave scale to demonstrate the principle. Start with a nearly full bottle of water and keep emptying out a little at a time. Encourage the students to notice what is happening to the sounds as the water level gets lower and more air enters the bottle. Explain that longer tubes of air vibrate more slowly and make lower pitched sounds.

Extend

Running a wet fingertip around the rim of a wine glass can produce a very clear sound. By altering the volume of water in each glass you can vary the pitch. Over 400 classical pieces of music have been written for this instrument!

I wonder...

Ask the students to place their fingertips gently on their throat when they speak. They should feel vibrations. In humans, sound is produced by the opening and closing of two thin strips of tissue in the back of our throats called the vocal cords. When the vocal cords are relaxed, the gap between them opens. When they are tightened, the gap closes. Opening the vocal cords produces a low-pitched sound; pulling them closed makes a high-pitched sound. As you get older, your vocal cords get bigger and so your voice deepens.

Dig deeper

Students should find out more information on the differences between light and sound and how they both travel.

Did you know?

These facts illustrate that very loud sounds can be harmful to your ears.

Other ideas

Make a sonic banger

Ask students to cut a square of card and a slightly larger square of brown wrapping paper. They

should cut the wrapping paper in half to make a triangle and glue this securely as shown below. Then fold the card and paper from corner to corner and flick the banger downwards through the air. The brown paper 'envelope' will flick out and make a loud bang.

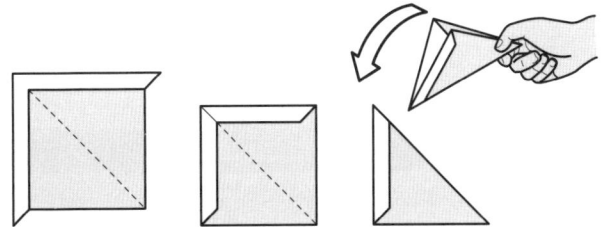

Sound challenge

Challenge the students to make as many different sounds as they can just using a paper cup, a piece of string, water and a piece of kitchen paper.

Presentation

In groups, invite the students to make up a story to tell as a radio play. Ensure that they incorporate several sound effects and atmospheric music. Let them record their play for the rest of the class to listen to.

At home

Ask the students to listen to a play or part of a serial on the radio or on cassette tape. *How many sound effects can you spot? Can you work out if the sound effects are real recordings or are artificially made?*

Plenary

Make a tape of everyday sounds in isolation, e.g. a door slamming, a hole punch, flicking through the pages of a book, pulling a tissue from a box, opening a drinks can, etc. Use the tape in a quiz. *How many sounds can you guess correctly?*

129

New International Edition

Unit 7: Sound – Unit 7 Review

The objectives for this lesson are that students should be able to:

- Check what they have learned about sound in this Unit

- Find out how they are working towards, within and beyond the Grade 4 level.

SB
p.102

Expectations

Students working towards Grade 4 level will:

- Suggest ways of producing sounds

- Recognize that hearing is one of our senses and we hear through our ears

- Distinguish between pitch and loudness

- Suggest how to change the sound made by an instrument

- Recognize that the further away you are from a sound the quieter it is and vice versa.

In addition, students working within Grade 4 level will:

- Generalize that sounds are produced when objects vibrate

- Suggest how to change the pitch and loudness of the sounds produced by a range of musical instruments

- Recognize that sounds travel through solids, water and air

- Suggest ways to investigate how well sound travels through different materials

- Say how good their evidence is

- Use evidence to communicate what was found out.

Further to this, students working beyond Grade 4 level will also:

- Describe ways in which the pitch of a sound made by a particular instrument or vibrating object can be raised or lowered

- Identify what is vibrating in a range of musical instruments.

Check-up

Hannah needs to retune her guitar. She needs to tighten the strings so that they vibrate at the correct frequency to produce the notes she needs when she plays an open string. Because the strings on a guitar are of different thickness, they need not all be tightened the same amount. Hannah can check the pitch of the string by comparing it with the note produced by a piano or a tuning fork.

Assessment

WS 76

Use the Unit 7 assessment on WS 76 to check the students' understanding of the content of the Unit. The answers are given opposite.

Name: _____ Date: _____

WS 76 Unit 7 assessment

1 Ali and Khaled use a tape recorder to play some music. Khaled played the music at different volumes. Ali recorded how far away she could hear the sounds. Here are their results.

Volume of tape recorder	1	2	3	4	5	6
Distance sound heard (m)	2	3	5		15	20

a) What material did the sound travel through to reach Aden's ears?

_____

b) Fill in the missing result on the table.

2 Class 4 were investigating soundproofing. They measured how close to a box they needed to be to hear a clock ticking. Different materials were added to the box each time. Here are their results.

Materials	Empty box	Scrunched up paper	Bubble wrap	Carpet
Distance sound heard (m)	2.75	0.80	1.10	0.50

Which material was the best at soundproofing? _____

3 Match each of these instruments to the way their sound is made.

Violin	Clarinet	Drum	Harp	Recorder

Vibrating string	Vibrating air in a tube	Vibrating skin

4 Riya has two elastic bands stretched over a tissue box. One is thicker than the other. Which band will give the lowest note? How can Riya make the thick elastic band make a higher note?

_____

_____

76   Heinemann Explore Science Grade 4

Answers

1 **a** Air
   b 10 m +/−1 m

2 Carpet

3 Violin → Vibrating string
   Clarinet → Vibrating air in a tube
   Drum → Vibrating skin
   Harp → Vibrating string
   Recorder → Vibrating air in a tube

4 The thick band
   Make it tighter/stretch it or make it thinner

The answer!

Discuss that Tariq's drums can be heard because of the way sound waves travel through different materials. The students could approach his problems from a couple of directions – making the initial sound quieter, by not putting so much energy into creating the sound or by using softer, more sound-absorbent materials to create the sound; secondly, stopping the sound from travelling so far by surrounding the room with sound-absorbing materials. Some students might remember that sound loses its energy over distance, so putting Tariq away from everybody else in a shed at the bottom of the garden might also be a solution!

And finally...

Encourage the whole class to make a musical composition using all of the elements of sound they have investigated.